Understanding Literature

DEREK SOLES
Wichita State University

Upper Saddle River
New Jersey 07458

Library of Congress Cataloging-in-Publication Data

Soles, Derek.
    The Prentice Hall pocket guide to understanding literature

        p. cm.
    Includes index.
    ISBN 0-13-026994-8
        1. English literature—History and criticism—Handbooks,
    manuals, etc.   2. American literature—History and criticism—
    Handbooks, manuals, etc.   3. Literature—History and
    criticism—Theory, etc.—Handbooks, manuals, etc.
    4. Literature—Terminology—Handbooks, manuals, etc.
    I. Title: Understanding literature.   II. Prentice-Hall, Inc.
    III. Title.
    PR21 .S64 2002
    808—dc21   2001021510

Editor in Chief: *Leah Jewell*
Senior Acquisitions Editor: *Carrie Brandon*
Editorial Assistant: *Thomas DeMarco*
Managing Editor: *Mary Rottino*
Production Liaison: *Fran Russello*
Editorial/Production Supervision: *Kim Gueterman*
Prepress and Manufacturing Buyer: *Sherry Lewis*
Cover Director: *Jayne Conte*
Cover Designer: *Bruce Kenselaar*
Cover Art: Henri Matisse, "Composition, fond bleu."
    Courtesy of Dr. Jakob Bill © 2000 Succession H. Marisse,
    Paris/Artists Rights Society (ARS), New York
Copyeditor: *Joan Eurell*
Marketing Manager: *Rachel Falk*

To Kate

This book was set in 8/11 Serifa Roman by ElectraGraphics, Inc.
and was printed and bound by R. R. Donnelley & Sons Company.
The cover was printed by Phoenix Color Corp.

© 2002 by Pearson Education, Inc.
Upper Saddle River, New Jersey 07458

For permission to use copyrighted material, grateful
acknowledgment is made to the copyright holders starting
on page 169, which are hereby made part of this copyright page.

Printed in the United States of America
10 9 8 7 6 5 4 3 2 1

ISBN 0-13-026994-8

Prentice-Hall International (UK) Limited, *London*
Prentice-Hall of Australia Pty. Limited, *Sydney*
Prentice-Hall Canada, Inc., *Toronto*
Prentice-Hall Hispanoamericana, S.A., *Mexico*
Prentice-Hall of India Private Limited, *New Delhi*
Prentice-Hall of Japan, Inc., *Tokyo*
Pearson Education Asia Pte. Ltd., *Singapore*
Editora Prentice-Hall do Brasil, Ltda., *Rio de Janeiro*

Contents

PREFACE xi

INTRODUCTION: WHAT IS LITERATURE? 1
Samuel Taylor Coleridge, *Kubla Khan* 1

1 FICTION 5
The Short Story **5**
    Frank O'Connor, *Guests of the Nation* **6**
    Elizabeth Tallent, *No One's a Mystery* **6**
    Jamaica Kincaid, *What I Have Been Doing Lately* **7**
    John Updike, *The A & P* **8**
    Raymond Carver, *Neighbors* **8**
The Novel **9**
    Jane Austen, *Pride and Prejudice* **9**
The Novella **11**
    Kate Chopin, *The Awakening* **11**

2 POETRY 13
Poetry: Regular Verse **13**
    William Wordsworth, *A Slumber Did
      My Spirit Seal* **15**
    William Blake, *The Tyger* **15**
    Lord Byron, *The Destruction of Sennacherib* **15**
    Ralph Hodgson, *Eve* **16**
    Gerard Manly Hopkins, *God's Grandeur* **17**
    Wilfred Owen, *Anthem for Doomed Youth* **17**
Poetry: Blank Verse **18**
    Alfred, Lord Tennyson, *Ulysses* **18**
Poetry: Free Verse **18**
    Matthew Arnold, *Dover Beach* **19**
    Wallace Stevens, *Disillusionment of Ten o'Clock* **19**
The Sonnet **20**
    William Shakespeare, *When in Disgrace
      with Fortune* **20**
    William Shakespeare, *Not Marble
      Nor the Gilded Monuments* **21**
    John Milton, *On His Blindness* **21**
    William Butler Yeats, *Leda and the Swan* **22**

The Ballad **22**
  Samuel Taylor Coleridge, *The Rime
    of the Ancient Mariner* **23**
  Dudley Randall, *The Ballad of Birmingham* **24**
The Villanelle **25**
  Dylan Thomas, *Do Not Go Gentle* **25**
The Ode **26**
  John Keats, *Ode to a Nightingale* **26**
  William Wordsworth, *Ode: Intimations
    of Immortality* **27**
The Epic **28**
  John Milton, *Paradise Lost* **28**
The Elegy **29**
  W. H. Auden, *In Memory of W. B. Yeats* **29**
The Dramatic Monologue **30**
  Alfred, Lord Tennyson, *Tithonus* **30**

3 DRAMA 31
Drama: Tragedy **31**
  William Shakespeare, *Hamlet* **32**
Drama: Comedy **34**
  Oscar Wilde, *The Importance of Being Earnest* **34**
Drama: Theater of the Absurd **35**
  Samuel Beckett, *Waiting for Godot* **35**

4 PLOT 38
The Sequential Plot **38**
  Katherine Mansfield, *The Garden Party* **38**
  Adrienne Rich, *Living in Sin* **39**
  Alice Munro, *The Found Boat* **39**
The Nonsequential Plot **40**
  William Faulkner, *A Rose for Emily* **40**
  Andre Dubus, *The Curse* **41**
  Carolyn Kizer, *Bitch* **42**
  Stephen Dixon, *All Gone* **42**
The Archetypal Plot **43**
  Joseph Conrad, *Heart of Darkness* **44**
  Robert Frost, *Directive* **45**
The Plot Twist **45**
  James Thurber, *The Catbird Seat* **46**
  Elizabeth Bishop, *The Fish* **46**
Plot and Irony **47**
  Thomas Hardy, *The Ruined Maid* **47**
  Laurie Colwin, *An Old-Fashioned Story* **47**
  Maxime Kumin, *Woodchucks* **48**
  William Shakespeare, *Othello* **49**

5 CHARACTER 51
Dynamic Characters **51**
    D. H. Lawrence, *The Odor of Chrysanthemums* **52**
    Herman Melville, *Bartleby, the Scrivener* **53**
    Sherwood Anderson, *I'm a Fool* **54**
Static Characters **54**
    T. S. Eliot, *The Love Song of J. Alfred Prufrock* **54**
    Katherine Mansfield, *Her First Ball* **55**
Stereotypical Characters **56**
    Robert Browning, *My Last Duchess* **56**
    F. Scott Fitzgerald, *The Great Gatsby* **57**
    Samuel Beckett, *Krapp's Last Tape* **58**
    Katherine Ann Porter, *The Jilting
      of Granny Weatherall* **59**
Character and Irony **59**
    Edwin Arlington Robinson, *Richard Cory* **60**
    Eudora Welty, *A Worn Path* **60**
    William Shakespeare, *Two Loves I Have of Comfort
      and Despair* **61**
Character and Satire **61**
    George Bernard Shaw, *Pygmalion* **61**
    Alice Walker, *Everyday Use* **62**
    Kurt Vonnegut, *Harrison Bergeron* **63**

6 POINT OF VIEW 65
The Omniscient Narrator **65**
    D. H. Lawrence, *The Rocking Horse Winner* **66**
    Kate Chopin, *The Storm* **66**
    Stephen Crane, *The Bride Comes to Yellow Sky* **68**
The Limited-Omniscient Narrator **68**
    James Joyce, *Eveline* **68**
    F. Scott Fitzgerald, *Babylon Revisited* **69**
First-Person, Major-Character Narrator **70**
    Margaret Atwood, *Rape Fantasies* **70**
    Alice Munro, *Boys and Girls* **71**
    Robert Hayden, *Those Winter Sundays* **72**
First-Person, Minor-Character Narrator **73**
    Doris Lessing, *Our Friend Judith* **73**
The Objective Narrator **74**
    Ernest Hemingway, *Hills Like White Elephants* **74**
Multiple Points of View **74**
    Charles Dickens, *Bleak House* **75**

7 SETTING 77
Setting and Plot **77**
    Sinclair Ross, *The Painted Door* **77**

William Trevor, *Beyond the Pale* **78**

Robert Browning, *Porphyria's Lover* **79**

Setting and Symbolism **80**

Robert Frost, *Stopping by Woods
on a Snowy Evening* **80**

Earnest Hemingway, *The Snows of Kilimanjaro* **81**

William Blake, *London* **81**

Setting and Irony **82**

Henry Reed, *Naming of Parts* **82**

Shirley Jackson, *The Lottery* **82**

T. S. Eliot, *The Waste Land* **83**

Setting and Metaphor **85**

William Shakespeare, *Full Many
a Glorious Morning* **85**

Thomas Hardy, *The Darkling Thrush* **86**

Yvor Winters, *At the San Francisco Airport* **86**

William Shakespeare, *A Midsummer
Night's Dream* **87**

8 THEME 90

Family **90**

St. Luke, *The Parable of the Prodigal Son* **90**

Theodore Roethke, *My Papa's Waltz* **91**

Katherine Mansfield, *The Daughters
of the Late Colonel* **92**

Richard Wilbur, *The Writer* **92**

Jamaica Kincaid, *Girl* **93**

Amy Tan, *Two Kinds* **93**

Sharon Olds, *The Planned Child* **94**

Love **95**

Elizabeth Barrett Browning, *How Do I Love Thee* **95**

Leonard Cohen, *Dance Me to the End of Love* **95**

E. E. Cummings, *somewhere i have
never travelled* **95**

William Butler Yeats, *The Folly
of Being Comforted* **96**

D. H. Lawrence, *The Horse Dealer's Daughter* **96**

War **97**

Wilfred Owen, *Futility* **97**

Denise Levertov, *What Were They Like* **97**

Tim O'Brien, *The Things They Carried* **98**

Randall Jarrell, *The Death of the Ball
Turret Gunner* **99**

Joseph Heller, *Catch 22* **99**

Irene Zabytko, *Home Soil* **101**

Richard Eberhart, *The Fury
of Aerial Bombardment* **102**

Nature **102**

John Keats, *To Autumn* **102**

A. J. M. Smith, *The Lonely Land* **103**

Maxine Kumin, *Morning Swim* **103**

Emily Dickinson, *I Taste a Liquor* **104**

Death **104**

William Butler Yeats, *Sailing to Byzantium* and
Byzantium **104**

John Donne, *Death Be Not Proud* **105**

William Shakespeare, *Poor Soul the Center of My
Sinful Earth* **105**

Dylan Thomas, *A Refusal to Mourn* **105**

Emily Dickinson, *Because I Could Not Stop
for Death* **106**

Faith **106**

John Donne, *Batter My Heart, Three-Personed God* **106**

Philip Larkin, *Church Going* **107**

George Herbert, *The Collar* **107**

Wallace Stevens, *Sunday Morning* **108**

Time **109**

Robert Herrick, *To the Virgins to Make Much
of Time* **109**

A. E. Houseman, *Loveliest of Trees* **109**

Edna St. Vincent Millay, *What Lips My Lips
Have Kissed* **110**

Denise Levertov, *A Time Past* **110**

9 METAPHOR 111

Metaphor and Character **111**

William Shakespeare, *That Time of Year Thou Mayest
in Me Behold* **112**

Stevie Smith, *Not Waving, But Drowning* **112**

James Joyce, *Clay* **112**

John Donne, *The Flea* **113**

Metaphor and Theme **114**

John Donne, *A Valediction:
Forbidding Mourning* **114**

W. S. Merwin, *Separation* **115**

John Keats, *On First Looking
into Chapman's Homer* **115**

Edgar Allan Poe, *The Masque of the Red Death* **115**

William Shakespeare, *My Mistress's Eyes Are
Nothing Like the Sun* **116**

Metaphor and Symbolism **116**

William Blake, *A Poison Tree* **116**

Robert Frost, *Desert Places* **117**

Emily Dickinson, *There's a Certain Slant of Light* **117**

10 IMAGERY 118

Imagery and Plot 118
  Ambrose Bierce, *An Occurrence
    at Owl Creek Bridge* 118
  A. D. Hope, *Imperial Adam* 119

Imagery and Character 120
  Diane Ackerman, *Beija Flor* 120
  Lord Byron, *She Walks in Beauty* 120
  James Joyce, *The Dead* 120
  Ben Jonson, *Still To Be Neat* 121

Imagery and Setting 122
  Dylan Thomas, *Fern Hill* 122
  Evelyn Waugh, *Brideshead Revisited* 122
  Marge Piercy, *Wellfleet Sabbath* 124

Imagery and Theme 124
  William Carlos Williams,
    The Red Wheelbarrow 124
  Ezra Pound, *In a Station of the Metro* 125

11 SYMBOLISM 126

Objects as Symbols 126
  Emily Dickinson, *My Life Had Stood
    a Loaded Gun* 126
  Sylvia Plath, *Mirror* 127
  John Keats, *Ode on a Grecian Urn* 127

Natural Symbols 128
  Robert Frost, *Fire and Ice* 128
  Emily Dickinson, *I Heard a Fly Buzz* 128
  William Blake, *The Sick Rose* 129
  Dylan Thomas, *The Force that
    through the Green Fuse* 129
  John Steinbeck, *The Chrysanthemums* 129

Religious Symbols 130
  James Joyce, *Araby* 130
  William Butler Yeats, *The Second Coming* 131

Character as Symbol 131
  John Cheever, *The Swimmer* 132
  Eudora Welty, *Livvie* 132
  Nathaniel Hawthorne, *Young
    Goodman Brown* 133

12 TONE 135

Sorrow 135
  William Butler Yeats, *When You Are Old* 135
  John Keats, *Bright Star* 136
  Katherine Mansfield, *Miss Brill* 136

Contents

Resignation **137**
   Nikki Giovanni, *Woman* **137**
   William Shakespeare, *When My Love Swears that
     She is Made of Truth* **137**
Irony **138**
   Dorothy Parker, *One Perfect Rose* **138**
   Lorrie Moore, *How To Become a Writer* **138**
   Wilfred Owen, *Dulce et Decorum Est* **139**
Triumph **139**
   G. K. Chesterton, *The Donkey* **139**
   Stephen Dunn, *Tenderness* **139**

13 THE AUTHOR'S LIFE AND TIMES 141
Personal Experience **141**
   Richard Lovelace, *To Althea, From Prison* **141**
   William Butler Yeats, *Among School Children* **142**
   John Milton, *Methought I Saw My Late
     Espoused Saint* **143**
Values and Ideals **143**
   Richard Lovelace, *To Lucasta, On Going
     to the Wars* **143**
Observed Experience **145**
   Alexander Pope, *The Rape of the Lock* **145**
Historical Circumstance **146**
   John Milton, *On the Late Massacre
     at Piedmont* **146**

14 AN INTRODUCTION TO METHODS OF LITERARY ANALYSIS 148
Formalism **148**
   John Keats, *La Belle Dame Sans Merci* **149**
Structuralism **150**
   Stephen Crane, *The Blue Hotel* **151**
Psychoanalytic Criticism **152**
   Henry James, *The Turn of the Screw* **153**
   Edgar Allan Poe, *The Cask of Amontillado* **153**
Archetypal Criticism **154**
   William Faulkner, *Barn Burning* **155**
Reader-Response Criticism **155**
   Emily Dickinson, *I Like to See It Lap the Miles* **156**
Marxist Criticism **157**
   Tillie Olsen, *I Stand Here Ironing* **158**
   Allen Ginsberg, *A Supermarket in California* **158**
Feminist Criticism **159**
   Bobbie Ann Mason, *Shiloh* **159**
   Andrew Marvel, *To His Coy Mistress* **161**
   Kate Chopin, *The Story of an Hour* **162**

Gay/Lesbian Criticism **162**
    Willa Cather, *Paul's Case* **163**
Deconstruction **163**
    William Wordsworth, *Daffodils (I Wandered Lonely
       as a Cloud)* **164**
    Flannery O'Connor, *A Good Man Is Hard to Find* **165**
New Historicism **166**
    Charlotte Perkins Gilman, *The Yellow Wallpaper* **167**
    Amy Tan, *A Pair of Tickets* **168**

CREDITS 169

AUTHOR-TITLE INDEX 173

LITERARY TERMS INDEX 179

Preface

The Prentice Hall Pocket Guide to Understanding Literature is a book for students who want to get a top grade in their college literature classes. It is a brief, straightforward guide to reading and understanding poetry, fiction, and drama.

To succeed in your literature classes, you must know the definitions of the various literary genres and sub-genres. These definitions are presented in Chapters 1, 2, and 3. You must also learn to recognize and discuss the elements of literature: plot, character, point of view, setting, theme, metaphor, imagery, symbolism, and tone. These literary elements are covered in Chapters 4 through 12. You also need to know how a writer's life and times can influence his or her work: biographical and contextual influences are covered in Chapter 13. Finally, you need to know the basics of contemporary literary criticism and theory. Chapter 14 reviews traditional critical approaches to literature and introduces some important contemporary approaches.

To illustrate the information covered in each chapter, *The Prentice Hall Pocket Guide to Understanding Literature* discusses, within an appropriate literary context, 116 poems, 61 short stories, 8 novels, and 7 plays. I have deliberately selected those poems, stories, and plays that most frequently appear on reading lists in undergraduate literature classes.

The Pocket Guide is, in short, a dictionary of literary terms, a guide to understanding a wide variety poems, stories, and plays that are frequently taught and anthologized, and an introduction to literary theory and criticism. I hope that it will help you do well in your literature course and make the course more interesting and relevant.

Derek Soles

Introduction: What Is Literature?

Literature is a form of oral and/or written expression that exploits the artistic dimension of language to entertain and enlighten readers. Here are two versions of the same text. One is literature; the other is not.

KUBLA KHAN

In Xanadu, did Kubla Khan A stately pleasure dome decree: Where Alph, the sacred river, ran Through caverns measureless to man Down to a sunless sea. So twice five miles of fertile ground With walls and towers were girdled round: And there were gardens bright with sinuous rills, Where blossomed many an incense-bearing tree; And here were forests ancient as the hills, Enfolding sunny spots of greenery. But oh! that deed romantic chasm which slanted Down the green hill athwart a cedarn cover!	The Emperor, Kubla Khan, built a magnificent palace in Xanadu. The Alph River flowed near the palace through dark and mysterious caves and out to sea. Ten miles of fabulous fragrant gardens encircled the palace. It was an enchanted palace where Kubla Khan heard voices and saw visions. Once I was inspired by a muse to write poetry as beautiful as the gardens of Xanadu.

KUBLA KHAN (continued)

A savage place! as holy and enchanted
As e'er beneath a waning moon was haunted
By woman wailing for her demon lover!
And from this chasm, with ceaseless turmoil seething,
As if this earth in fast thick pants were breathing,
A mighty fountain momently was forced:
Amid whose swift half-intermitted burst
Huge fragments vaulted like rebounding hail,
Or chaffy grain beneath the thresher's flail:
And 'mid these dancing rocks at once and ever
It flung up momently the sacred river.
Five miles meandering with a mazy motion
Through wood and dale the sacred river ran,
Then reached the caverns measureless to man,
And sank in tumult to a lifeless ocean:
And 'mid this tumult Kubla heard from far
Ancestral voices prophesying war!
  The shadow of the dome of pleasure
  Floated midway on the waves;
  Where was heard the mingled measure
  From the fountain and the caves.
It was a miracle of rare device,

If I could get that inspiration back, I would write beautiful poetry again.

I would become a powerful force, capable of changing the world.

People would be in awe of me.

KUBLA KHAN (continued)

A sunny pleasure dome with caves of ice!

A damsel with a dulcimer
In a vision once I saw:
It was an Abyssinian maid,
And on her dulcimer she played,
Singing of Mount Abora.
Could I revive within me
Her symphony and song,
To such a deep delight
'twould win me,
That with music loud and long,
I would build that dome in air,
That sunny dome! those caves of ice!
And all who heard should see them there,
And all should cry, Beware! Beware!
His flashing eyes, his floating hair!
Weave a circle round him thrice,
And close your eyes with holy dread,
For he on honeydew hath fed,
And drunk the milk of paradise.
　　　—Samuel Taylor Coleridge

Obviously, the text on the left, the poem, is literature. It is true that both texts are a form of written expression and both enlighten readers. But what about the third component of our definition of literature, "exploits the artistic dimension of language"? The prose summary is plain and simple; the poem is creative and artistic. The prose version is a house plant compared to the colorful garden of the poem. Coleridge uses vivid imagery, rich vocabulary, rhythm, rhyme, and metaphor to augment and intensify the message he is presenting. The prose summary is not striking or memorable; the poem is.

It is the use of language, then, that distinguishes literature from other forms of written expression. The language of a poem is different from the language of a business letter, a textbook, or a newspaper. Similarly, the language in a story or a play tends to be more creative and artistic than the letters or the newspaper articles that we read. Storytellers rely on tone, vivid diction, and imagery to establish their settings and describe their characters. A play is primarily spoken language or dialogue, but the spoken language in a play tends to be more elevated, more carefully crafted, than ordinary conversation. Some plays, Shakespeare's for example, are even written almost entirely in verse.

To a poet, a playwright, and a storyteller, language is more than a medium of communication. It is also an art form. A writer uses language in much the same way as an artist uses shape and color, to share with the reader/observer the artist's vision of a dazzling landscape, a colorful character, a transforming experience, or an intense emotion.

Fiction

The first task of a student of literature is to learn the definitions and the characteristics of the major literary categories or genres. There are three main literary genres: fiction, poetry, and drama. In this chapter fiction is defined and discussed. In the next two chapters, poetry and drama are defined and discussed.

Fiction is prose text in the form of a story that is primarily a product of human imagination. There are three forms of fiction: the short story, the novella, and the novel.

THE SHORT STORY

A short story is a prose fiction narrative. Prose is the "everyday" written text of the daily newspaper, textbooks, and letters. Fiction, though it might be based in reality, is primarily a creation of the imagination, as opposed to a factual reporting of true experience. A narrative is a description of a significant experience in a person's life.

In a short story, the experience usually occurs in a single setting, and concerns a single main character, the story's **protagonist.** Other characters will challenge or support the protagonist as he or she experiences the events that comprise the story. One of these characters will usually block or vex the aspirations of the main character. The character who blocks or vexes the main character is known as the **antagonist.** The protagonist usually learns from the experience he or she undergoes throughout the story, although occasionally he or she misses the opportunity to do so. A short story might consist of only a few paragraphs or of many pages, but it won't be so long that an average reader could not read it in less than two hours.

Frank O'Connor, Guests of the Nation

"Guests of the Nation" is a typical short story, often studied in school and college literature classes. The guests referred to in the title are two English soldiers, Hawkins and Belcher. They are actually prisoners of war, the 1916 war between Great Britain and Ireland. However, because they bond with their captors and show no interest in escape, they become more like guests than enemies. They play cards with their captors, converse as equals, and help out with the chores around the house, in Ireland, where the story is set. When word comes of the execution of Irish prisoners held by the British, Hawkins and Belcher's guards are ordered to execute their prisoners in retaliation. No one can believe the absurd situation in which he finds himself. Belcher even offers to change sides. But this is war, and in war the absurd becomes commonplace. The guests of the nation are executed.

The narrator of the story is a young Irish soldier named Napoleon, and his experience guarding two men whom he gets to know and whom he then must execute transforms him. While he does not put his thoughts into so many words, he comes to understand the irrationality of settling disputes by executing innocent men, and, in a broader context, the irrationality of war, especially between two peoples who have so much in common. He realizes, as the story comes to an end, that he has changed, that from now on he will see the world and his place in it in a different light.

This change in the main character's values or ideals, often occurring at the end, is a typical element of a short story. This change, this sudden insight or awareness revealed to the main character, is sometimes referred to, in literary criticism, as an **epiphany.**

Elizabeth Tallent, No One's a Mystery

In some stories, the main character is offered an opportunity to grow and mature, but refuses or is unwilling to do so. In other words, she refuses the epiphany her experiences present to her. "No One's A Mystery" is such a story.

The story is very brief, only several pages long. It takes place one summer afternoon, in a time span of under an hour, in a truck driving down a Wyoming highway. The narrator has just turned eighteen and her married boyfriend, Jack, has given her a diary for her birthday. The two of them drive around aimlessly and speculate on what the narrator will be writing in her diary in a few years. Jack claims the diary entries will eventually depict him as a distant memory, a fling along the narrator's road to adulthood.

The narrator, by contrast, imagines Jack will divorce his wife, marry her, and settle down to raise a family with her. Most readers are left with the impression that Jack's version of the future is closer to the truth, that the narrator is living in a fantasy world of a Harlequin romance.

Despite its brevity, "No One's A Mystery" is a story that has been told many times before about a relationship between a single young woman and a considerably older married man. It is also a story about contrasting characters, one a romantic, the other a realist. In the end, the realist seems to prevail. He urges the narrator to realize the true nature of their relationship, but she is too starstruck to do so. His last seven words to her ring with irony. Correcting her romantic misconception about how their baby will smell, Jack says: "And her breath would smell like your milk, and it's kind of a bittersweet smell, *if you want to know the truth.*" The truth is exactly what the young narrator does not want to know.

Jamaica Kincaid, What I Have Been Doing Lately

In her story, "What I Have Been Doing Lately," Jamaica Kincaid challenges the conventions of the short story genre.

The plot is both surreal and circular or, perhaps more accurately, spiricular. The narrator is lying in bed, hears the doorbell, answers it, finds no one, and goes for a walk. She sees the planet Venus and a monkey in a tree, before she comes to a body of water she cannot cross. Years pass, and then she gets into a boat and rows across. She continues her walk and encounters ordinary objects that become extraordinary: a boy with a ball that becomes flowering trees, a hole she deliberately falls down and then commands to close. Her journey seems interminable.

A figure approaches her. At first, she thinks it is her mother, but it turns out to be a stranger. The woman asks her, "And just what have you been doing lately?" She considers some bizarre responses, then answers by retelling the story of her walk, but retelling it with details now changed. The monkey, harmless in the story's first iteration, now throws a rock at the narrator, causing a gash in her forehead that immediately heals. She crosses the water on a ferry boat. On the other side are beautiful "black and shiny people" who metamorphose into mud. The narrator continues to walk, exhausted now. She wants to get back home and she hopes to find her mother there, making her a custard. She wishes it were Sunday and she were listening to someone singing a psalm. Tired and full of sorrow, the narrator, at the end of the story, goes "back to lying in bed, just before the doorbell rang."

What is the reader to make of such an unconventional plot that defies the traditions of the typical short story? Readers must use some creativity and imagination in interpreting unconventional literary works. Perhaps Kincaid is sharing with us an actual dream she had—certainly the story has a dream-like quality to it. Perhaps "What I Have Been Doing Lately" is metaphorical (see Chapter 9), and the episodes in the story represent the journey through life, which does often seem unplanned, unpredictable, bizarre, and puzzling. The ending of the story supports this possibility, describing as it does that universally human hope and search for love and faith.

John Updike, The A & P

"The A & P" is a story about a young man, a grocery clerk, who quits his job, after his manager embarrasses a group of young women who enter the grocery store, improperly dressed (in the manager's opinion) in bathing suits. The young man's decision is spontaneous. Apparently he hopes to win the young women's admiration, to be their hero, but they don't even turn around after he makes his dramatic announcement, and he soon realizes he will regret his rash actions.

The style of Updike's story might come as a surprise to readers who expect literature to be "literate," to be written in proper English. Updike does not begin his story by writing: One summer day, three young women, wearing nothing but bathing suits, walked into the grocery where I work. Instead, he writes: "In walks these three girls in nothing but bathing suits." This casual style is maintained throughout the story.

Updike's purpose is to add authenticity to his story and to give readers insight into its main character, the young clerk Sammy, by telling the story in Sammy's voice. The story may not be a lesson in good grammar but it does effectively reflect the personality and character of its narrator. He is a nineteen-year-old man, working at a quite menial job that obviously does not bring him much satisfaction. He wants more out of life; he wants to do significant things, to be noticed. Ironically, the young women he staunchly defends and for whom he sacrifices his job, pay no attention to him.

Short story writers can break the rules if, by doing so, they enhance the artistic integrity of their work. By telling the story from Sammy's point of view, Updike makes his story more true-to-life and entertaining.

Raymond Carver, Neighbors

"Neighbors" is also an unconventional story, though in this case it is the characters and the action and not the style that is unconventional. Indeed, the style is very simple and straightforward, even pedestrian. It works well, in that it intensifies the aberrant behavior the two main characters exhibit.

The Millers and the Stones live across the hall from each other. The Stones go away often and the Millers look after the Stones' apartment and cat, while they are away. The Millers envy the Stones who seem to have a more active and interesting life than they have. Indeed, looking after their neighbors' apartment is an event in the Millers' lives, and they make the most of it. Bill Miller even calls in sick one day, so he can study the contents of his neighbor's apartment in minute detail. He puts on Jim Stone's Hawaiian shirt and Bermuda shorts, drinks the neighbor's liquor, and puts on one of Jim's suits. Then he puts on Harriet Stone's underwear, a skirt, and a blouse. The experiences unleash a weird passion between Bill and Arlene Miller, and they are excited about the prospect of making love on their neighbors' bed. They are making plans to do so, when they realize they forgot the keys in their neighbors' apartment after they left the night before, and now they are locked out. They cling to each other in fear, as the story comes to an end.

Involving as it does intense prying, cross-dressing, and other unusual behavior, "Neighbors" is a somewhat unconventional story. On one level it is about that typical human feeling that others must be living more stimulating, interesting, exciting, fulfilled, and passionate lives than we are. In the case of the Millers, however, the feeling is actually correct. On another level, then, "Neighbors" is about losing touch with reality, a condition that might be brought on by the tedious life the Millers seem to lead and by their sense of social isolation.

THE NOVEL

A novel has the same characteristics as a short story but is, of course, longer. An average reader would need at least four hours to read a novel. To describe the characteristics of a typical novel, we basically turn the singular nouns of the short story into plural nouns. A novel is a prose fiction narrative, but, unlike the short story, it usually recounts significant experiences in the lives of interesting characters in a variety of settings. A novelist has the luxury of a more leisurely unfolding of plot and development of character, and novels tend to be less intense than short stories.

Jane Austen, Pride and Prejudice

In *Pride and Prejudice,* for example, Jane Austen tells the story of not one but three romances that develop over a period of at least a year, in several different locales. Her main focus is the development of the relationship between Elizabeth Bennett and Fitzwilliam Darcy. Elizabeth is initially not attracted to Darcy who she regards as a pompous snob. Darcy is attracted to Elizabeth, however, even though he feels she is beneath him socially. He proposes to her and is stunned to be rejected, apparently believing Elizabeth would be honored by his interest in her. Thereafter, he realizes he has behaved badly and he begins to reconsider and change his ways. Elizabeth, too, comes to realize she had prejudged Darcy, that he is more reserved than arrogant, and she accepts him when he next proposes. He is the pride of the title, and she is the prejudice. After the usual series of misunderstandings and miscommunications, they realize they are perfect for each other, that they complete each other: He needs her to soften his stiff demeanor and improve his social graces; she needs him to learn the restraint and tolerance expected of a woman of her social status.

Counterpoised to the Elizabeth/Darcy relationship are two very different ones. Elizabeth's sister, Jane, loves Darcy's friend Bingley, and he loves her. But Darcy convinces his friend that Jane is beneath him socially and advises Bingley against pursuing the relationship. After Elizabeth convinces Darcy of the error of his ways, he admits to Bingham he was wrong and encourages him to propose to Jane.

Another sister, Lydia, causes scandal by eloping with the dashing young army officer, Wickham. Wickham was one of the most popular of the officers in town, a favorite, even, of Elizabeth. But his social graces and good looks hide a disreputable character, which is eventually revealed. He had no intention of marrying Lydia, but is forced to by Darcy who has known him all his life and who feels some responsibility because he failed to alert the Bennett family to the true nature of Wickham's character.

Typical of a great novel, *Pride and Prejudice* is full of wonderful minor characters who support or harass or put roadblocks in the way of the main characters. Mrs. Bennett is the perfect scheming mother, doing whatever it takes, willing to make a fool of herself, to help her five daughters find suitable husbands. The Bennett girls' cousin, Reverend Collins, is a wonderful comic character, an unctuous social climber who flatters, with complete insincerity, anyone he thinks might benefit him. The major recipient of his annoying flattery is the haughty Lady Catherine de Borough, Darcy's aunt, who tries to block the marriage between his nephew and Elizabeth, but who, unwittingly, brings them together. So, too, does Bingham's sister who wants Darcy for herself and who therefore never misses an opportunity to criticize Elizabeth behind her back, an activity that only forces Darcy to defend Elizabeth and make him more aware of his love for her.

Pride and Prejudice is typical of the "happily-ever-after" novel. At the end, those who deserve good fortune and happiness have it, and those who do not, do not.

THE NOVELLA

A novella is longer than a short story but shorter than a novel. As such, it typically contains more characters, more settings, and more actions than a short story, but fewer than a novel.

Kate Chopin, The Awakening

The Awakening, for example, is half the length of an Austen novel, containing thirty-nine short chapters, compared to the sixty-one chapters divided into three volumes of *Pride and Prejudice.*

Set in the 1890s, *The Awakening* is the story of Edna Pontellier, who is on vacation with her husband, Leonce, and family at a resort on Grand Isle on the Gulf Coast. Edna is, at first, depicted as the conventional wife and mother in this upper-class, southern family. She is the property of her husband and assumes the role of the conventional, privileged wife and mother. However, she is vaguely aware of a dissatisfaction with her domestic situation, an awareness that will grow throughout the story and, ultimately, transform her.

Her transformation is induced by two friends and a lover. One friend is Adele Ratignolle who is the perfect wife and mother, content to suppress her own needs and aspirations, in favor of those of her husband and children. Edna sees in Adele a self-sacrifice she, herself, admires but is unable to make. The other friend is Mlle. Reisz, the owner of a Grand Isle boarding house, a woman who has chosen to remain unmarried and independent. Edna admires her but cannot identify with Mlle. Reisz's celibacy; indeed, it is Edna's sensuality that, in part, evokes her desire for change.

The lover, the man who awakens this sensuality, is a young Creole man, Robert Lebrun. Robert loves and leaves Edna, whose growing independence and self-assertion begin to disconcert him. The experience of forbidden love amidst the sensuous Gulf Coast setting awakens Edna's desire for a less confined and conventional life.

When her holiday is over, she returns to her home in New Orleans' French Quarter, but she cannot resume the roles of wife and mother her society expects her to assume. Leonce tries to help her but is frustrated by her detachment and leaves on a business trip without her when she refuses to accompany him. She has an affair with a neighbor, Alcee Arobin. Robert visits her but leaves the same day, making it clear they have no future together. She attends to Adele, as Adele has another baby.

These events coalesce into Edna's realization that she has changed and can no longer cope with the life she is expected to lead. She returns alone to Grand Isle, takes off all her clothes and swims out into the Gulf, apparently with no intention of returning to a life with so many restraints she can no longer accept.

The Awakening is a story about the relationship between the individual and her society, a subject often at the center of works of fiction. Edna and the world in which she lives are out of sync. She wants liberation, but social forces forbid it.

The southern setting of the novella, especially the languorous warm breezes, the sunshine, and the ocean of the Gulf Coast, influence Edna's transformation. Here her senses come alive and she begins to realize she does not have to conform. Here, also, she learns to swim and, in the process, discovers a physical strength that parallels and reinforces her new emotional strength and rebelliousness.

With its memorable characters, romantic setting, and story of a young woman struggling against social barriers to find her own identity, *The Awakening* is part of a rich fictional tradition that includes Flaubert's *Madame Bovary,* much of the work of the Brontë sisters, and Tolstoy's *Anna Karenina.*

Poetry

Poetry is usually written, occasionally oral, text that accents the metaphorical, imagistic, rhythmic, and other aural properties of language and that, unlike prose, is usually shaped into discrete lines of equal or unequal length. There are three main divisions of poetry: regular verse, blank verse, and free verse. There are seven other verse forms: the sonnet, the ballad, the villanelle, the ode, the epic, the elegy, and the dramatic monologue. Each of these poetic forms is defined and described in this chapter.

POETRY: REGULAR VERSE

A regular verse poem is a literary work written in lines that have the same rhythm pattern and a regular rhyme scheme. If a regular verse poem is divided into stanzas or verse paragraphs, each stanza will have the same number of lines. A two-line stanza is called a **couplet.** (If the last words in each line rhyme, it is called a **rhyming couplet**). A three-line stanza is called a **tercet;** a four-line stanza is called a **quatrain;** a six-line stanza is called a **sestet;** and an eight-line stanza is called an **octave.**

Each stanza in a regular verse poem will have the same pattern of rhyme. The rhyming pattern of a regular-verse poem is called the **rhyme scheme.** Regular verse poems have a recurring rhyme scheme. The last word in alternate lines might rhyme, the last word in each pair of lines might rhyme, or there may be some other recurring pattern. A rhyme scheme is described by assigning the same small letter to each end-of-line word that rhymes with another end-of-line word. For example, a rhyme scheme described as *aabb* means that the last words in each pair of lines rhyme; a rhyme scheme of *abab* means the last words in alternate lines rhyme. Any pattern is acceptable as long as it recurs. In most of his odes, for example, John Keats used the rhyme scheme *ababcdecde* for each of his ten-line stanzas.

There are various degrees of rhyme. **Full rhyme** refers to words that rhyme completely: *good wood*. **Eye** or **sight rhymes** are words that look like they should rhyme but do not: *good mood*. **Half rhyme** (sometimes called partial, imperfect, off, or slant rhyme) refers to words that sound somewhat alike: *home alone.*

There are four regular verse **rhythm patterns: iambic, trochaic, anapestic,** and **dactylic.** A regular-verse rhythm pattern might be interrupted, by a pattern used only on occasion, notably the **spondee.**

The **iambic** rhythm pattern consists of one unstressed sound or beat followed by one stressed sound or beat. The unstressed sound is represented by a "smile line": ⌣. The stressed sound is represented by an angled line: /. Each line of a regular verse iambic poem will have the same number of beats. A line with two beats—I saw a bird—is called **iambic dimeter;** a line with three beats—I saw a bird up in—is called **iambic trimeter;** a line with four beats—I saw a bird up in the sky—is called **iambic tetrameter;** a line with five beats—Today I saw a bird up in the sky—is called **iambic pentameter.** Iambic meter is the most common poetic meter, suggesting that lilting quality we tend to associate with poetry.

William Wordsworth, A Slumber Did My Spirit Seal

Here is an example of a classic regular verse iambic poem, "A Slumber Did My Spirit Seal" by William Wordsworth:

> A slumber did my spirit seal;
>   I had no human fears;
> She seemed a thing that could not feel
>   The touch of earthly years.
>
> No motion has she now, no force;
>   She neither hears nor sees;
> Rolled round in earth's diurnal course,
>   With rocks, and stones, and trees.
>   (1800)

This poem, one of several Wordsworth wrote about a young woman named Lucy who apparently died prematurely, is written in alternating lines of iambic tetrameter (the odd-numbered lines) and iambic trimeter (the even-numbered lines). Its rhyme scheme is *abab, cdcd.*

Trochaic meter is the opposite of iambic. The rhythm of the lines of a trochaic poem consist not of a series of soft-stress-hard-stress sounds but a series of hard-stress-soft-stress sounds. While iambic has a lilting quality, trochaic is harder, more energetic. Trochaic meter pounds upon the page.

William Blake, The Tyger

William Blake chose the trochaic meter for his poem "The Tyger" because he wanted to communicate the sense of energy and force that a tiger exudes. To Blake, a tiger is fierce, threatening, deadly, but still beautiful, a symbol of the forceful aspect of God's nature, in contrast to the gentleness of the lamb. Notice, in the first two stanzas of this eight-stanza poem, how the pounding trochaic meter reinforces the tiger's fiery energy:

> Tyger! Tyger! burning bright
> In the forests of the night,
> What immortal hand or eye
> Could frame thy fearful symmetry?
>
> In what distant deeps or skies
> Burnt the fire of thine eyes?
> On what wings dare he aspire?
> What the hand dare seize the fire?

"The Tyger" is written in trochaic tetrameter with an *aabb ccdd eeff*, etc., rhyme scheme.

The **anapestic** meter consists of a series of two unstressed sounds followed by a single stressed sound: ⌣⌣/. It gives the impression of quick movement.

Lord Byron, The Destruction of Sennacherib

Because the anapestic meter suggests quick movement, Byron chose the anapestic for his poem "The Destruction of Sennacherib," in which he describes the attack on Jerusalem by a huge army of Assyrian soldiers under the command of King Sennacherib. Notice how the anapestic tetrameter meter heightens the sense of the violent movement of an attacking army:

> The Assyrian came down like the wolf on the fold,
> And his cohorts were gleaming in purple and gold;

˘ ˘ / ˘ ˘ / ˘ ˘ / ˘ ˘ /
And the sheen of their spears was like stars on the sea,

˘ ˘ / ˘ ˘ / ˘ ˘ / ˘ ˘ /
When the blue wave rolls nightly on deep Galilee.

Like the leaves of the forest when summer is green,
That host with their banners at sunset were seen:
Like the leaves of the forest when autumn hath blown,
That host on the morrow lay withered and strown.

(1815)

The balance of Byron's eight-stanza poem describes the defeat of Sennacherib's army by divine intervention. An angel of God confronts the Assyrians and destroys them all in order to protect the holy city of Jerusalem.

The **dactylic** meter is the opposite of the anapestic. It consists of a series of a single hard-stressed sound followed by two soft-stressed sounds: /˘˘. The dactylic meter is something of a novelty in English poetry. It is overtly rhythmic and

/ ˘ ˘ /
is frequently used in children's verse: Home again, home
˘ ˘ / ˘ ˘ /
again, jiggity jig.

Ralph Hodgson, Eve

"Eve" is a rare example of a sedate use of dactylic meter. The poem describes the temptation of Eve by Satan in the form of a serpent. The serpent follows Eve around the Garden, then speaks to her. Eve pauses before she acts:

/ ˘ ˘ / ˘ ˘
Picture that orchard sprite,
/ ˘ ˘ / ˘ ˘
Eve, with her body white,
/ ˘ ˘ / ˘ ˘
Supple and smooth to her
/ ˘ ˘ /
Slim finger tips,
Wondering, listening,
Listening, wondering,
Eve with a berry
Half-way to her lips.
(lines 25–32)

The ingenuous Eve falls, of course, and is expelled from the Garden. In this poem, the dactylic meter is very effective in creating a pastoral but faintly ominous atmosphere, which complements the poem's action.

Varied rhythm and meter. Many regular-verse poems contain lines or phrases that vary the poem's rhythm pattern.

Gerard Manley Hopkins, God's Grandeur

"God's Grandeur" begins with two iambic feet:

$$\smile \quad / \quad \smile \quad /$$
The world is charged

then switches to anapestic:

$$\smile \quad \smile \quad / \quad \smile \quad \smile \quad /$$
with the grandeur of God.

Note how the sudden switch to anapestic intensifies the "charging" effect that the poem describes.

The next line continues the anapestic meter until the last two words, both of which are hard-stressed:

$$\smile \quad \smile \quad / \quad \smile \quad \smile \quad / \quad \smile \quad \smile \quad / \quad /$$
It will flame out, like shining from shook foil;

The double-hard-stressed phrase "shook foil" is called a **spondee.** Poets will use a spondaic rhythm pattern on occasion, usually for emphasis.

Notice, as well, the repetition of the "sh" sound in the above line. Repetition of a consonant sound is called **alliteration.** Poets will use alliteration to create a particular effect. In the line above, the alliteration suggests the very sound shook foil would likely make.

"God's Grandeur" continues with a somewhat mixed rhythm and meter. Hopkins' theme is that the beauty of nature is a manifestation of God's presence on earth, and that natural beauty will survive despite the way humans exploit nature for their own economic gain.

Wilfred Owen, Anthem for Doomed Youth

"Anthem for Doomed Youth" begins with two iambic pentameter lines that describe the slaughter of young First World War soldiers whose deaths are commemorated not by the ringing of funeral bells but by the "monstrous anger of the guns." The next two lines read:

Only the stuttering rifles' rapid rattle
Can patter out their hasty orisons.

Notice how the iambic pentameter rhythm is interrupted with the alliterative r's of "rifles' rapid rattle," which actually imitate the sound of gunfire. This is enhanced by the repetition of the "a" sound in "rapid rattle" and "patter." This repetition of vowel sounds is known as **assonance.**

POETRY: BLANK VERSE

Blank verse is easily defined: It is unrhymed iambic pentameter poetry. Each line of a blank verse poem has five soft-stress-hard-stress beats, but the last words of the lines rhyme only coincidentally. Blank verse conveys a formal, authoritative tone. It is quite similar to prose yet it has the aura of poetry. It is familiar, yet elevated language. Shakespeare chose blank verse as the language of his plays; John Milton chose it for his great epic, *Paradise Lost*. Blank verse has an exalted history in English literature.

Alfred, Lord Tennyson, Ulysses

Tennyson chose blank verse for his poem "Ulysses" because the poem is in the form of a speech Ulysses gives to his crew, and blank verse is the poetic form that approximates ordinary human speech, while, at the same time, conveying an elevated and formal tone.

Ulysses was the King of Ithaca, a hero of the Trojan War, and the subject of one of Homer's great epic poems, *The Odyssey.* After many years of adventure, Ulysses returns home to his wife, Penelope, and his son Telemachas. Homer ends the story at this point, but Tennyson picks it up and continues. He depicts Ulysses as a man incapable of settling down with his family, eager to set out again on an adventure, despite his advancing years. He addresses his crew, urging them to come with him and "drink life to the lees" (line 6). By presenting Ulysses' speech in blank verse, Tennyson conveys the sense that a great man is speaking. Ulysses explains his inability to settle down, his desire to continue his journey despite the dangers. He knows he and his crew still have the strength and the will to explore the world some more:

> Though much is taken, much abides; and though
> We are not now that strength which in old days
> Moved earth and heaven, that which we are, we are:
> One equal temper of heroic hearts,
> Made weak by time and fate, but strong in will
> To strive, to seek, to find, and not to yield.
> (lines 65–70)

POETRY: FREE VERSE

Free verse is poetry without a set rhyme scheme or rhythm pattern. There might be rhyme in a free verse poem and there will be rhythm. But there is no repetitive rhythm as there is in regular verse and blank verse and no repetitive rhyme scheme as there is in regular verse.

Matthew Arnold, Dover Beach

"Dover Beach" is a much-studied free-verse poem. It was written in the middle of the nineteenth century, at a time of social unrest. Reform-minded English people were beginning to criticize the brutal working conditions even children had to endure in the mines and factories. Scientists like Charles Darwin were casting doubt upon biblical explanations of the origin of life.

In "Dover Beach," Arnold hears the ocean waves beneath the white cliffs of Dover and compares the ebb and flow of the ocean tides to the ebb and flow of religious faith. The tide of faith is ebbing, he claims, in such a confused and uncertain world:

> The Sea of Faith
> Was once, too, at the full, and round earth's shore
> Lay like the folds of a bright girdle furled.
> But now I only hear
> Its melancholy, long, withdrawing roar,
> Retreating to the breath
> Of the night wind, down the vast edges drear
> And naked shingles of the world.
> (lines 21–28)

The irregular line lengths and irregular rhyme indicate the free verse structure. Notice how the free verse form helps to establish the melancholy, pensive tone of the poem and how the irregular rhythm helps convey the sound of the "long, withdrawing roar" of the retreating tide.

As the poem comes to an end, the poet pledges his love for the woman he is with and begs for truth between them as an antidote to the sorrow, violence, pain, and confusion that currently pervade the world.

Wallace Stevens, Disillusionment of Ten o'Clock

The speaker in this poem is disillusioned because he lives in a white, unimaginative world. Even our dreams, the speaker says, have become unimaginative. Only the indigent, he seems to imply, have the gift of a vivid imagination. Note, in these lines that end the poem, how Stevens uses diction and imagery, as opposed to rhythm, rhyme, and meter, to give his work a poetic voice:

> People are not going
> To dream of baboons and periwinkles.
> Only, here and there, an old sailor,
> Drunk and asleep in his boots,

Catches tigers
In red weather.
(lines 10–15)

THE SONNET

A sonnet is a fourteen-line regular-verse poem, usually written in iambic pentameter. As a regular verse poem, it has, of
course, a regular rhyme scheme. There are two main types
of sonnet distinguished from each other by their rhyme
scheme.

William Shakespeare, When in Disgrace with Fortune

The **Shakespearean sonnet** has an *ababcdcdefefgg* rhyme
scheme. Study carefully the form of the following sonnet,
Sonnet 29, by William Shakespeare:

When in disgrace with Fortune and men's eyes,
I all alone beweep my outcast state,
And trouble deaf heaven with my bootless cries,
And look upon myself and curse my fate,
Wishing me like to one more rich in hope,
Featured like him, like him with friends possessed,
Desiring this man's art and that man's scope,
With what I most enjoy contented least;
Yet in these thoughts myself almost despising,
Haply I think on thee, and then my state
(Like to the lark at break of day arising
From sullen earth) sings hymns at heaven's gate;
    For thy sweet love remembered such wealth brings
    That then I scorn to change my state with kings.

Notice how the rhyme scheme defines sections of the sonnet,
dividing the fourteen lines into four quatrains and a rhyming
couplet. The first four lines (*abab*) describe the poet's despair. The next four (*cdcd*) tell what the poet envies in others but doesn't have himself. The next four (*efef*) indicate
how the poet relieves his despair by remembering his friend's
love. The last two lines form a rhyming couplet; that is, the
last words in both lines rhyme: "brings" "kings." As is typical of sonnets by Shakespeare, the last lines summarize the
sonnet and best express its theme: I realize how lucky I am
when I remember I have your love.

William Shakespeare, Not Marble Nor the Gilded Monuments

In Sonnet 55, "Not Marble Nor the Gilded Monuments," Shakespeare maintains his usual form, though he uses more half rhymes ("masonry/memory" and "enmity/prosperity") than he typically does.

The sonnet concerns one of his favorite subjects: the immortality of poetry. When all is gone, the poet tells his friend: After monuments have toppled and war has destroyed the earth, you will live on, immortalized in the sonnets I write in praise of your character.

John Milton, On His Blindness

The other main type of sonnet, the **Petrarchan sonnet,** has an *abbaabbacdecde* rhyme scheme. The rhyme scheme divides the fourteen lines into one octave (an eight-line stanza) and one sestet (a six-line stanza). The break between the two stanzas is not necessarily indicated by a line space.

Here is an example of a Petrarchan sonnet, John Milton's famous poem, "On His Blindness":

> When I consider how my light is spent,
>> Ere half my days in this dark world and wide,
>> And that one talent which is death to hide
>> Lodged with me useless, though my soul more bent
> To serve therewith my Maker, and present
>> My true account, lest he returning chide;
>> "Doth God exact day-labor, light denied?"
>> I fondly ask; but Patience to prevent
> That murmur, soon replies, "God doth not need
>> Either man's work or his own gifts; who best
>> Bear his mild yoke, they serve him best. His state
> Is kingly. Thousands at his bidding speed
>> And post o'er land and ocean without rest:
> They also serve who only stand and wait."
>
> (1673)

Milton went blind in 1651, at the age of 43. In this sonnet, he wants to complain about the injustice and sense of irony he feels. God gave him the talent to write poetry yet has denied him the light he needs to express that talent. Before he can utter his complaint, however, he senses the voice of God telling him to be patient. God will let the poet know what He expects from Milton as He will with all of those who serve Him. In the meantime, "They also serve who only stand and wait."

Because of its brevity, the sonnet is well suited to express specific, pointed themes. "On His Blindness" is a good example of the sonnet as an effective medium for the expression of a succinct yet eloquent sentiment.

Many poets have written sonnets that **combine the Shakespearean and Petrarchan** forms or that display a unique rhyme scheme while, of course, staying within the fourteen-line iambic pentameter form that distinguishes the sonnet from other poetic forms.

William Butler Yeats, Leda and the Swan

In "Leda and the Swan," for example, William Butler Yeats builds a sonnet out of two Shakespearean quatrains followed by a Petrarchan sestet. The sonnet describes the rape of the Spartan Queen Leda by the Greek god Zeus, who assumed the form of a swan and violated the beautiful young Queen. Yeats describes the rape in the sonnet's first eight lines.

In the sestet, he considers the profound consequences of the rape. As a result of the union between Leda and Zeus, Leda gave birth to Helen of Troy. Helen eventually married Menelaus but was seduced by the Trojan, Paris, who took her back home to Troy. Menelaus and his brother Agamemnon, the King of Mycenae, attacked Troy to get Helen back. The rape of Leda caused, at least indirectly, the ten-year Trojan War.

Agamemnon was married to Clytemnestra, Helen's sister, and when he returned home victorious to Mycenae, Clytemnestra killed him so she would not have to give up her lover.

To Yeats, the rape of Leda by Zeus was a cataclysmic event, an annunciation, which marked the beginning of Greek civilization. Yeats' sonnet is atypical in its historical sweep. He manages, in the sestet, to summarize the Trojan War, tell of the death of Agamemnon, and offer a topical comment on the abuse of power.

THE BALLAD

A ballad is a narrative poem, usually written in quatrains, which often have an alternating iambic tetrameter, iambic trimeter meter and an *abcb* rhyme scheme. In narrative poems, ballad writers often make use of dialogue to advance their stories. Ballads also frequently contain supernatural occurrences. They usually have specific themes or morals, which the author usually presents explicitly at the end.

Samuel Taylor Coleridge, The Rime of the Ancient Mariner

The most famous ballad in the language, "The Rime of the Ancient Mariner," by Samuel Taylor Coleridge, exemplifies all the characteristics of the ballad form. It is written in quatrains, which alternate (with an occasional variation) between iambic pentameter and iambic trimeter and it uses the *abcb* rhyme scheme, as the opening two stanzas illustrate:

It is an ancient Mariner
And he stoppeth one of three.
—"Bye thy long gray beard and glittering eye,
Now wherefore stopp'st thou me?

The Bridegroom's doors are opened wide,
And I am next of kin;
The guests are met, the feast is set:
May'st hear the merry din."

As Coleridge's long ballad continues, the ancient mariner gets his way and compels the wedding guest to listen to his story. The mariner tells of an ocean voyage, interrupted by a storm, which drives the ship to the South Pole. An albatross appears to guide the ship, but the mariner impulsively kills the bird with his crossbow. His fellow sailors ostracize him and hang the dead albatross around his neck. The crew falls upon hard times. Another ship approaches and the crew is hopeful until they realize with horror that the ship is a skeleton operated by Death and Life-in-Death. With the appearance of these two characters, Coleridge introduces that element of the supernatural common in ballads. The two ghastly characters roll dice to determine the fate of the crew. Death wins the crew who begin to drop dead; Life-in-Death wins the ancient mariner.

The mariner suffers as if he were in hell. Then he turns his attention to God's creatures swimming in the ocean below him. He thinks how beautiful they are, and he subconsciously blesses them. Having thus reestablished his respect for nature, the mariner is rewarded; his penance ends:

A spring of love gushed from my heart,
And I blessed them unaware:
Sure my kind saint took pity on me,
And I blessed them unaware.

That self-same moment I could pray;
And from my neck so free

> The Albatross fell off, and sank
> Like lead into the sea.
> (Part 5, lines 284–291)

Rain comes, the dead crew temporarily comes back to life, inhabited by the spirits of angels, and the mariner makes it back to England. As part of his punishment and rehabilitation, he is compelled to tell his story to people like the hapless wedding guest who the mariner senses will most benefit from his tale of the dire consequences that threaten those who do not respect nature. The ballad's ending is typical of the genre in that it ends with a specific statement of the poem's theme:

> He prayeth best, who loveth best
> All things both great and small;
> For the dear God who loveth us,
> He made and loveth all.

> The Mariner, whose eye is bright,
> Whose beard with age is hoar,
> Is gone: and now the Wedding-Guest
> Turned from the bridegroom's door.

> He went like one that hath been stunned,
> And is of sense forlorn:
> A sadder and a wiser man,
> He rose the morrow morn.
> (Part 7, lines 614–625)

Dudley Randall, The Ballad of Birmingham

We might think of the ballad as an old and traditional poetic form but, in fact, ballads continue to be written. Dudley Randall's "The Ballad of Birmingham" was published in 1966, three years after the episode that inspired it occurred. In 1963, a bomb went off in a Birmingham church, killing four black children.

The ballad begins with the voice of one of the children, asking her mother if she can participate in the freedom march to be held that day in Birmingham. The mother refuses, afraid for her daughter's safety. The march, a pro-civil rights event, could turn into a riot. Instead, the mother urges her daughter to go to church and sing in the choir. The child does so and, horribly ironically, is killed when the bomb blows the church apart.

Randall's ballad does not contain that element of the supernatural common in traditional ballads. However, it does contain the dialogue, the rhythm pattern, and the *abcb* rhyme scheme typical of the ballad form:

"Mother dear, may I go downtown
Instead of out to play;
And march the streets of Birmingham
In a Freedom March today?"

The poem is characterized also by the heartbreaking sense
of irony—the little girl dies in church, where she did not really want to be—also common in ballads.

THE VILLANELLE

A villanelle is a nineteen-line poem divided into five tercets
(three-line stanzas) and one quatrain (a four-line stanza). It
has a very specific structure. It has an iambic pentameter
rhythm and meter and an *aba aba aba aba aba abaa* rhyme
scheme. The first line of the first tercet of a villanelle is repeated as the last line of the second and fourth tercets. The
last line of the first tercet is repeated as the last line of the
third and fifth tercets. These two lines, the first and third of
the first tercet, form a rhyming couplet at the end of the poem.

Dylan Thomas, Do Not Go Gentle

"Do Not Go Gentle Into That Good Night" is undoubted-
ly the most frequently anthologized villanelle in the language.
In the poem, Thomas urges his dying father, a gentle man, to
fight death:

Do not go gentle into that good night,
Old age should burn and rave at close of day;
Rage, rage against the dying of the light.
(lines 1–3)

Notice how the iambic rhythm is broken by the powerful
spondee "Rage, rage" in the third line.

Thomas goes on to describe stereotypical men—wise
men, good men, wild men, and grave men—in stanzas two
through five respectively, explaining to his father how they
all regretted something about the way they lived their lives
and, as a result, resented death and fought against it. In
keeping with the villanelle format, the last lines of the second and fourth tercets are identical to the poem's opening
line; the last lines of the third and fifth are identical to the last
line of the first tercet.

As the poem comes to an end, Thomas urges his father to
follow the leads of those wise, good, wild, and grave men,
and fight against death:

And you, my father, there on the sad height,
Curse, bless, me now with your fierce tears, I pray.

Do not go gentle into that good night.
Rage, rage against the dying of the light.
(lines 16–19)

THE ODE

An ode is a long formal poem that usually presents a poet's philosophical views about such subjects as nature, art, death, and human emotion. Most odes are written in regular verse; some are in free verse.

John Keats, Ode to a Nightingale

John Keats's odes are among the most famous **regular-verse odes** in the language. "Ode to a Nightingale" is a typical Keats ode. It is a poem of 80 lines, divided into 8 stanzas of 10 lines each. The lines have an iambic pentameter rhythm (broken in line 8 by a line of iambic trimeter) and an *ababcdecde* rhyme scheme.

Odes often concern the relationship between the human and natural worlds. Keats addresses this ode to a nightingale whose song symbolizes the permanence of nature, in contrast to the impermanence of human existence. The ode describes the poet's desire to escape from a life that is filled with hardship and join the nightingale in the peaceful, beautiful, and eternal world that resonates with its own incomparable song. Keats wanted so much to share in such a world because his own was so tragic. He was terminally ill with tuberculosis, an illness that had already taken his young brother, Tom. Keats alludes to Tom's death in stanza 3, wherein he describes the sorrow and brevity of life as he knows it:

Where youth grows pale, and spectre-thin, and dies;
  Where but to think is to be full of sorrow
    And leaden-eyed despairs,
Where beauty cannot keep her lustrous eyes,
  Or new love pine at them beyond to-morrow.
(Stanza 3, lines 26–30)

Understandably, he longs for a place without pain and suffering and thinks he can find it within the nightingale's mystical realm. He reaches that place and it turns out to be all he had hoped for. In stanzas 5 and 6, Keats describes the intoxicating scent of the flowers, the ecstatic song of the nightingale, and the sense of immortality he feels there.

But he knows his escape is only temporary. As the nightingale's song fades, the poet is jolted back to reality. "The fancy cannot cheat so well / As she is famed to do," he says in the final stanza. He is left somewhat disoriented by the whole intense experience.

"Ode to a Nightingale," typical of its genre, is a contemplation on life and death, the human and the natural. Also typical of the English ode is its reflective tone, tinged with sorrow and resignation.

William Wordsworth, Ode: Intimations of Immortality

While most odes are written in regular verse, a few are in free verse. The most famous **free-verse ode** in English is William Wordsworth's "Ode: Intimations of Immortality." It is a 203-line poem divided into 11 stanzas of various length and rhythm. Wordsworth uses rhyme extensively within each stanza but the poem does not have a repetitive rhyme scheme.

Wordsworth begins his poem by reflecting on his past, specifically the joy he experienced as a child communing with nature. Now, as an adult, that spontaneous joy has passed and he yearns to get it back. For several stanzas, 4 through 8, Wordsworth celebrates the beauty and innocence of childhood, a time of freedom and innocence bolstered by a naïve belief in immortality.

Inevitably, though, the innocence of childhood gives way to the responsibility of adulthood. Adulthood is burdensome compared to the freedom of childhood, but Wordsworth does not dwell on the negative. Instead, he finds comfort in remembrance of things past:

> Though nothing can bring back the hour
> Of splendour in the grass, of glory in the flower;
> We will grieve not, rather find
> Strength in what remains behind;
> In the primal sympathy
> Which having been must ever be;
> In the soothing thoughts that spring
> Out of human suffering;
> In the faith that looks through death,
> In the years that bring the philosophic mind.
> (Stanza 10, lines 177–186)

Wordsworth's "Immortality Ode" has the same quiet, philosophical, reflective tone as "Ode to a Nightingale" and, like Keats's ode, focuses on nature and the lessons we can learn by examining our relationship with the natural world. Wordsworth's ode is more upbeat than Keats's, however, ending as it does with the sense that the wonder of childhood has been superseded by a more mature and realistic view of life.

THE EPIC

An epic is a narrative poem, the length of a long novel. It has a traditional structure. An epic typically opens in the middle of the action (the literary term is **in medias res**), continues chronologically through several events, then flashes back to the beginning of the story, and finally jumps back to the point where the flashback began and continues the story to its conclusion.

Epic poems always include both mortal and supernatural characters who regularly interact. The poet begins by invoking a supernatural power to help him tell his story and has supernatural characters—gods, goddesses, angels—intervene in the lives of mortal characters either to help them achieve a goal or to thwart their plans and aspirations. A god, goddess, or angel will typically warn a mortal character before a cataclysmic event takes place.

The plot of an epic poem usually focuses on warfare, its causes and its consequences. Homer's great epic *The Iliad* describes the siege of Troy by Greece and her allies. *The Odyssey,* also by Homer, describes the adventurous voyage home after the Trojan War of Odysseus, King of Ithaca. Virgil's famous epic *The Aeneid* tells of Aeneas' escape from the Greeks at the end of the Trojan War and his harrowing journey to his homeland, Italy.

John Milton, Paradise Lost

In the English language, the great epic poem is John Milton's *Paradise Lost. Paradise Lost* opens in Hell where Satan announces to his fellow fallen angels that God is planning to create a whole new world. Satan and his followers agree that they can spoil God's plan and be avenged for their defeat by corrupting man who will inhabit God's new world. Satan sets out on the mission. He persuades Sin and Death to unlock the Gates of Hell so he can proceed. He tricks the archangel Uriel into revealing the location of the Garden of Eden. Disguised as a cormorant, he spies on Adam and Eve from the Tree of Life at the edge of the Garden. He learns about the Tree of Knowledge on which grows the forbidden fruit.

The archangel Gabriel learns of Satan's presence in the Garden and sends three angels to protect Adam and Eve. Satan leaves, but not before putting a dream in Eve's consciousness about the pleasure of tasting the fruit of the forbidden tree. God sends his angel Raphael to warn them about

Satan and to remind them that He gave man free will, so
Adam and Eve might fall from grace. Raphael also tells them
the story of man's creation. Chronologically, the epic begins
at this point.

Satan returns to the Garden, assumes the form of a serpent, and tempts Eve to taste of the forbidden fruit. She does
so and convinces Adam to do the same. They have knowledge now of evil, and their personalities and actions change
accordingly. God sends his Son to the Garden to pass judgment on Adam and Eve. He forgives them but foretells a
bleak future. The archangel Michael arrives to lead them out
of the Garden. He offers them hope, as the epic ends, promising that the Son of God will come to earth to redeem man's
sins.

Paradise Lost, in keeping with the epic genre, tells the ultimate story: the battle between good and evil, more specifically the triumph of good over evil. The temptation to sin
is irresistible; if Adam and Eve were sinners, so are we all.
But because sin is redeemed through (in this epic) the Christian values of love, compassion, temperance, and devotion,
good will triumph in the end. Ultimately, Adam and Eve's ex-
pulsion from the Garden is less tragic than bittersweet, in
that they leave with the knowledge that faith in the Re-
deemer, who will come to earth one day, can lead them back
to Paradise.

THE ELEGY

An elegy is a poem written to commemorate the death of a
person who played a significant role in the poet's life. Famous elegies include Shelley's "Adonais" in memory of the
death of John Keats; Tennyson's "In Memoriam," written to
commemorate the death of his friend, Arthur Hallam; and
"Lycidas," Milton's homage to his friend Edward King. These
poets praise the virtues of their friends and often use the occasion of their friends' deaths to comment on the role fate
plays in an uncertain world. A **pastoral elegy** (such as "Adonais" and "Lycidas") typically contrasts the serenity of the
simple life of a shepherd with the cruel world that hastened
the death of the poet's friend.

W. H. Auden, In Memory of W. B. Yeats

"In Memory of W. B. Yeats" is the best-known elegy written in the twentieth century. This poem expresses sorrow,
tempered by the realization that Yeats will live on through his
work and the many readers who admire it. Typical of the
genre, this elegy contrasts Yeats' wisdom with the greed and

dispassion of the modern world. The poem was written on the eve of the Second World War:

> In the nightmare of the dark
> All the dogs of Europe bark,
> And the living nations wait,
> Each sequestered in its hate.
> (lines 46–49)

A poet's art, Auden suggests, transcends war's hate, heals the bruised soul, and lets "the healing fountain start" (line 63).

THE DRAMATIC MONOLOGUE

A dramatic monologue is a poem that is "dramatic" in the sense that it is a speech presented to an audience (sometimes of only one person) and a "monologue" in the sense that no other character does any talking. Some dramatic monologues, such as T. S. Eliot's "The Love Song of J. Alfred Prufrock," are written in free verse; some, like Robert Browning's "My Last Duchess," are in regular verse; and some, like Tennyson's "Ulysses," are in blank verse.

Alfred, Lord Tennyson, Tithonus

"Tithonus" is an important blank verse dramatic monologue by Alfred, Lord Tennyson. Tithonus was a Trojan prince loved by Aurora, the goddess of the dawn. Aurora wanted to have Tithonus forever, so she prayed to the gods to make Tithonus immortal. Her prayers were answered. Unfortunately, she did not ask that Tithonus be granted the gift of eternal youth. Tithonus grows so old and withered, he can no longer bear his life, and he begins to yearn to die. In this dramatic monologue, Tithonus asks Aurora to "take back thy gift" (line 27). He is surrounded by the matchless beauty of the universe, one of the advantages of being the roommate to the goddess of the dawn. Yet he wants to be a man again and "have the power to die" (line 70).

"Tithonus" is a dramatic monologue that validates the nature of the human life cycle, which culminates with the death of the body and the concomitant release of the spirit.

Drama

Drama is performance text, a story told through the dialogue of its characters and presented in front of a live audience. There are three main types of drama: tragedy, comedy, and theater of the absurd.

DRAMA: TRAGEDY

As a literary genre, a tragedy is a play that tells the story of a significant event or series of events in the life of a significant person. This person is called the **tragic hero.** The tragic hero is usually a man, though notable exceptions include Shakespeare's Cleopatra and Juliet, and Sophocles' Antigone. He is usually a member of the nobility: a king, a prince, or an emperor. He is well-respected within his community, a leader, a wise, just, and good man.

But the tragic hero is human, and, as such, is imperfect. The tragic hero has a character defect, called the **tragic flaw** or **hamartia.** He might be arrogant or too impulsive or indecisive or insecure. This flaw, whatever it is, causes many problems that snowball and ultimately result in catastrophe for the very community the tragic hero should be leading.

In keeping with this movement toward catastrophe, brought on by the tragic hero's hamartia, the plot of a tragedy tends to move from bad to worse because of the tragic hero's errors in judgment, even though the errors are unwitting. The disaster might be a plague, widespread civil unrest, or a general atmosphere of distrust and suspicion. The misplaced actions (or lack of action) of the tragic hero cause or contribute in a major way to the disaster. In a tragedy there is a general sense that the cards are stacked against the tragic hero and the world in which he lives, that he is the victim of a malign fate.

In the interests of the restoration of the community, the tragic hero must go. A tragedy will typically end with the death or the exile of the tragic hero. Thereafter, life in the community begins to get back on track. The tragic hero, then, is ultimately a scapegoat. A **scapegoat** is a person who is banished or sacrificed so that his or her community can continue to survive and prosper. Typically, the scapegoat atones in some way for his sins and for the sins of his people. The concept of sacrifice, of the *scapegoat,* is central to the definition of tragedy. The word tragedy comes from the Greek word meaning "goat's song."

Paradoxically, a tragedy is not, in the end, an occasion for sorrow, but more an occasion for relief. The audience witnesses disaster and despair acted out before them. They are moved to pity for the tragic hero and anger at a world that can seem to be so heartless. At the end of the play, the audience releases this pity and anger. They feel better, then, for having purged body, mind, and soul of pent-up emotions. This purgation of audience emotion is central to the theory of tragedy. It is known as the **catharsis**. Catharsis is not something that happens to the characters in the play; it is the very heavy collective sigh of both grief and relief the audience heaves, as the tragic hero is defeated and as, in the wake of that defeat, order returns to his world.

William Shakespeare, Hamlet

Hamlet is the most frequently taught and anthologized English tragedy. The plot of the play is typical of the genre in that fate seems to conspire against any possibility for harmony and happiness in the world the play inhabits.

Hamlet is the story of the murder of the King of Denmark, and the attempt by Prince Hamlet to avenge his father's murder. The murder was committed by Hamlet's own uncle, his father's brother, Claudius, who murdered the King to take over the throne and marry Queen Gertrude, Hamlet's mother. The murder devastates Hamlet, who falls into a depression and ends his relationship with his girlfriend, Ophelia. Hamlet agonizes over his duty to avenge his father's "foul and most unnatural murder," largely because he learned of the crime from the ghost of his father, and he is not at all sure he can trust the "word" of a ghost. He establishes Claudius's guilt, however, by tricking Claudius, in a most ingenious way, into revealing his guilt: He arranges for a theater company to stage a play that reenacts his father's murder; Claudius's obvious discomfort establishes his guilt.

Still, Hamlet's attempts at revenge are thwarted. He kills, by accident, his uncle's chief advisor, Polonius, Ophelia's father, and, as a result, the king sends him into exile. By now Claudius is certain Hamlet intends to kill him. Hamlet manages to get back to Denmark, however, to try again, thanks to the intervention of some friendly pirates. Polonius's son, Laertes, to avenge his father's death at the hands of Hamlet, challenges Hamlet to a duel and conspires with Claudius to poison his blade to effect Hamlet's death. In the course of the duel, both Hamlet and Laertes are wounded with the poisoned sword, and Laertes then reveals Claudius's treachery. Before the poison ends his life, Hamlet stabs Claudius and forces down his throat a glass of poisoned wine, meant for Hamlet, in the event that the poisoned sword did not work. Meanwhile, Gertrude has also died, having innocently drunk some of the poisonous wine. As the play ends, the new King of Norway arrives to restore order within the rotten state of Denmark.

Hamlet is the archetypal tragic hero. He is a handsome, intelligent young prince, an expert swordsman, and loved by the people of his country. His tragic flaw, however, is his lack of emotional balance. Hamlet's engine has two gears: stop and charge. He either acts rashly, without thinking, as he does when he kills Polonius and attacks Laertes at Ophelia's funeral, or he does not act expeditiously enough. He never gets around to killing Claudius and avenging his father's murder until the end of the play when it is really too late. Up until that point, Hamlet philosophizes about death, ponders the consequences of his actions, finds excuses to stonewall, and waxes poetic about all manner of subjects. He does not act quickly and expeditiously enough. Hamlet admires his friend Horatio because Horatio has that balance between reason and emotion Hamlet knows he needs but cannot attain. This lack of balance, especially his tendency to talk too much and act too slowly, defines Hamlet's tragic character and causes his downfall. Man is free to act, say the existentialists, but man must act to be free.

The imagery (see Chapter 10) in *Hamlet* reflects and augments the atmosphere of corruption and hypocrisy that pervades Denmark, governed as it is by a king who murdered his own brother. Images of decay and disease validate Bernardo's claim, early in the play, that "something is rotten in the state of Denmark." Images of concealment, of women hiding their true selves behind thick makeup, of "sugaring over the Devil himself," of outward appearance masking inward treachery highlight the hypocrisy that runs rampant throughout a kingdom where almost everyone is something other than what he or she appears to be.

The end of the play brings relief, catharsis, as a tragic ending must. Vicariously, we feel the characters' pain. We grieve at the deaths of Hamlet and Ophelia, accept the death of Claudius, and know that with the arrival of Fortinbras, literally "strong in arms," Denmark will return to the rule of law and good government.

DRAMA: COMEDY

Comedy is, in most ways, the opposite of tragedy. The plot of a comedy moves not from bad to worse but from bad to better, and ends in happiness for the characters who deserve it. Typically, in a comedy, young men and women want to come together but are prevented from doing so by a variety of obstacles, which range from bad luck to unyielding adults. In the end, though, the luck changes: Those who would block the union are thwarted, and the young people marry and, the audience is led to believe, live happily ever after.

In a tragedy the main characters are generally serious and solemn and one character, the tragic hero, dominates the action. In a comedy, the main characters remain upbeat no matter what fate brings them, sensing that in the end they will triumph. In a comedy, the characters tend to be **stereotypical,** which means they are recognizable *types* of people rather than fully developed characters like the tragic hero. Common stereotypical characters include the dumb blonde, the vain young man who thinks he is God's gift to women, the miser, the fickle young lover, the lazy slob, the embarrassing relative, the rich spoiled child, the social snob. Those characters who try to prevent the union of the young people are referred to as **blocking agents.**

The spirit or the tone of comedy is different from the spirit of tragedy. In a comedy, there is always a sense that everything will turn out well, despite the horrible predicaments the characters find themselves in. The setting, amusing dialogue, plot, and characters combine to establish the optimistic comic spirit.

Oscar Wilde, The Importance of Being Earnest

The Importance of Being Earnest is a much taught, much anthologized comedy. It is the story of two young men and two young women who want to get engaged but can't because circumstances stand in their way. Gwendolyn's mother, Lady Bracknell, won't let Gwendolyn marry John because John has no real family; he was, in fact, discovered in a train station as a baby and raised by a philanthropic country gentleman. Gwendolyn loves John, mainly because she thinks his name is actually Earnest, which is her favorite name. Only in a comedy could a character fall in love with a name, instead of with the person behind the name. John assumes this false identity when he comes to London.

The other couple in the play are Algernon and Cecily. Algernon wants to marry Cecily but can't because his best friend is her guardian and that friend who is, of course, John, thinks Cecily is too young and Algernon too experienced, so he refuses to agree to the union. Cecily falls in love with Algernon, even before she meets him, because she believes he is actually John's reprobate brother, who she believes is really a romantic adventurer. But the brother is, of course, John's fictitious creation who he has named (naturally) Earnest. Earnest, it turns out, is not only Gwendolyn's favorite name, but Cecily's as well. Algernon visits John's country house, pretending to be John's brother in order to meet and win Cecily. This is exactly what he does, to John's utter disapproval.

At this point, then, John cannot marry Gwendolyn because he has no family, and Algernon cannot marry Cecily because John forbids the match. Besides, both young women are furious when they discover they have been lied to and that neither one is engaged to an Earnest. But this is a comedy, and, in a comedy, such problems are transitory. With the help of Cecily's tutor, Miss Merriman, John's true identity is revealed. He is, of course, Algernon's older brother, and his real name is, of course, Earnest.

The characters in *The Importance of Being Earnest* are typical comic stereotypes. Lady Bracknell is the blocking agent, a hilariously supercilious meddlesome mother. John and Algernon are spoiled young aristocrats who don't have to work for a living and who spend their time dining at the right places, shopping for the right clothes, and flirting with eligible young women. Their counterparts are Gwendolyn and Cecily, fickle and superficial, frivolous, indulged, self-absorbed, rich, and spoiled young women.

Typical of a comedy, *The Importance of Being Earnest* makes us laugh with the witty banter and sarcasm the characters exchange. It has the ingredients of the classical comedies: mistaken identity, explained away at the end; an abandoned baby who turns out to be related to another character; young people whose energy and enthusiasm conquer anything that stands in the way of their happiness.

DRAMA: THEATER OF THE ABSURD

Theater of the absurd is a phrase used to describe a group of plays written during and after the 1950s. The term "absurd" is used because the plots and the characters (though not the themes) are unconventional when examined in the context of conventional tragedy and comedy. The characters are eccentric, and their speech and their actions often seem unintelligible. The plots are often static; any forward movement that does occur is usually reversed by the time the play ends. The themes are the predictable issue of the plot and characters, bleak in their obsession with the hopelessness of the human condition, yet intriguing and thought-provoking at the same time.

Samuel Beckett, Waiting for Godot

Waiting for Godot, which opened in Paris in 1953, is usually considered to be the first theater of the absurd play, and it remains one of the most widely anthologized and taught.

The play is set on a deserted road where two apparently homeless and derelict men, Vladimir and Estragon, are waiting for a third man, Godot, though they are not sure exactly why they are waiting for him. They talk about sore feet, they try to remember the story about the thieves executed with Christ, and they even consider hanging themselves from the one tree on their desolate road. They smile because "one daren't even laugh any more." They reach the conclusion: "Nothing to be done." They wait.

Two new characters, Pozzo and Lucky, arrive. Lucky has a rope around his neck and Pozzo is driving him forward using a whip. Vladimir and Estragon are in awe of Pozzo's power over Lucky. Pozzo orders Lucky to perform for them, specifically to "think." Lucky's famous "think speech" is, predictably, rambling and meaningless, though, typical of a theater of the absurd play, some statement about human faith or faithlessness does seem to struggle to emerge from between the lines. Pozzo and Lucky leave. A young boy enters with a message from Godot: He is not coming tonight, "but surely tomorrow." Vladimir and Estragon decide to go but do not move.

The opening of Act II, which apparently takes place the next day, is a recapitulation of Act I, except the tree now has a few leaves on it. Vladimir notices the change as the pair sit down to wait again for Godot. They are not sure if it is the same tree, if time has passed, or if they are in the same place. They reminisce about their days picking grapes in a beautiful valley so different from the wasteland they now inhabit. They find a hat, apparently belonging to Lucky, and play with it for a while. They call each other mean names, as a way of passing time. Estragon begs for God's pity. Pozzo and Lucky arrive on the scene again, this time in altered circumstances. Pozzo is blind and Lucky is mute, the rope is much shorter than it was in Act I, and Lucky carries suitcases full of sand. They fall down, and, in trying to help them back up, Vladimir and Estragon fall down as well. Eventually, Pozzo and Lucky struggle up and continue on their journey, and the other two are left alone with their despair once again. A messenger arrives with the news that Godot will not come this evening but will come tomorrow. They consider hanging themselves again but Estragon has forgotten the rope and the cord holding up his pants is too weak. They resolve to hang themselves tomorrow if Godot does not come. They decide to go but, again, do not move.

The main theme of *Waiting for Godot* is the loss of faith in the modern world and the human inability to find something to replace God(ot). Some people, like Vladimir and Estragon, wait for salvation; others, like Pozzo and Lucky, attempt to find faith in the material world instead—an attempt that exploits one of them and eventually grinds both of them, quite literally, down.

The breakdown of communication is another important theme of the play, evident in the characters' difficulty in sustaining a conversation with each other and in Lucky's parody of intellectual discourse. Paradoxically, and typical of a theater of the absurd play, there is much meaning in the characters' inability to find meaning in their lives, devoid as they are of faith, hope, and charity and drawn to the consideration of their own deaths. Theater of the absurd dramatists place characters in settings and situations that are, on the surface, absurd, but which represent real social issues that need to be addressed.

Plot

A story, a narrative poem, and a play are made up of a sequence of events. These events, the order in which they occur, and the relationship of the events to each other comprise the **plot** of the literary work. Writers usually present their plots in the temporal order in which the events occurred. This is known as a **sequential plot.** Sometimes authors will choose not to narrate the events in chronological order but will alter the time order to create suspense. Such a story has a **nonsequential plot.** A story that has a sequence of events familiar to readers because they have read or been told similar stories before has an **archetypal plot.** Writers (and readers) tend to prefer plots that are unpredictable. The surprise ending or the **plot twist** is a time-honored plot device. Events in a story will often unfold in a way opposite to the way we had expected they would. Such a story is said to have an **ironic plot.** In this chapter, each of these plot patterns is defined and described.

THE SEQUENTIAL PLOT

Life is a temporal sequence of events, so stories that mirror life are generally narrated chronologically, that is, in the order in which those events occur in time. Those events, their relationship to each other, and the order in which they are presented to the reader comprise the **plot** of a story, a play, or a narrative poem. A **sequential plot** is one in which the events are narrated in the order in which they occurred in time.

Katherine Mansfield, The Garden Party

Katherine Mansfield's classic story "The Garden Party," for example, begins on a fine summer morning and ends the evening of that same day. In between, the events that form the plot of the story occur. The well-to-do Sheridan family makes plans for an elaborate garden party to be held at their beautiful New Zealand home. They learn about the death of a neighbor, a young carter, killed when his horse shied at a tractor and threw its rider. A working man, the young carter lived in one of the row of poor cottages below the Sheridan's mansion. Laura, the only member of the Sheridan family who has anything of a social conscience, insists they cancel the party. Other members of her family can't imagine doing anything so extreme simply because a mere workman has died. Laura, too, relents when she sees how dazzling she looks in her new hat and how exciting it will be to show her beauty off to the garden party guests.

When the party is over, her guilty conscience returns. She takes a basket of sandwiches, left over from the party, to the widow and children of the dead man. Against her will, she is led into the room where the dead carter lies. She can think of only three words to say, "Forgive my hat." The words suggest that Laura's social conscience, implied earlier in the story, will continue to flourish.

Adrienne Rich, Living in Sin

"Living in Sin" is an example of a narrative poem with a sequential plot. The poem tells the story of a day in the life of a young woman who is living with her boyfriend. The poem begins the morning after the young couple have hosted a party, and it expresses the woman's bitterness over the state their apartment is in. She has defied convention by living with her boyfriend without first marrying him, and she had thought their love would transcend trivial everyday problems. But when he gets up and goes out for cigarettes, obviously expecting her to deal with the mess from the party, she is resentful. She loves him still but the experience has taught her that her knight's armor does not always shine.

Alice Munro, The Found Boat

"The Found Boat" is a good example of a story with a sequential plot that unfolds over a brief period of time, probably about two weeks. The story is set in a small Ontario town, a part of which floods every spring when the local river rises. Children of the town venture to the flooded parts to wade in the water and ride floating logs. Two girls, Eva and Carol, who are about twelve, discover a dilapidated old rowboat and tell a group of boys, who rescue the boat and decide to restore it. Over the course of a week or so, the boys restore the boat under the watchful eyes of Eva and Carol. When the repairs are complete, they carry the boat down to the river and take turns going for rides. They end up at an abandoned railway station. They eat their lunch inside, then play a game of truth or dare that ends with all of them naked and swimming in the river. One of the boys squirts water from his mouth onto Eva's breasts, she becomes self-conscious, and the fun ends. The boys and girls separate, and the story ends with the girls laughing uncontrollably.

"The Found Boat," then, contains five sequential episodes: the discovery of the boat, the repair of the boat, the launch of the boat, the game of truth or dare, and the skinny-dipping in the river. It is an exemplary well-made and straightforward coming-of-age story. It is a story of sexual awakening, of a group of boys and girls who are at once fascinated with and repelled by each other, as they display the typical gender rivalries of their age, even as they subconsciously realize that there is an intense bond between them.

THE NONSEQUENTIAL PLOT

While most stories are narrated in a chronological sequence, some authors will choose to hold back an important incident that occurred before the chronological ending of the story. In other words, the story will have a **nonsequential plot.** The advantage of a nonsequential plot is **suspense.** The author holds back an event because the plot of the story turns on that event. To reveal it earlier would diminish the story's impact, while to reveal it at the end, or out of chronological sequence, keeps the reader engaged in the story's plot. The technique of narrating an event that occurred before the point in the story to which the narrator has advanced is known as a **flashback.**

William Faulkner, A Rose for Emily

One of the most frequently taught stories with a nonsequential plot is William Faulkner's "A Rose for Emily." Chronologically, the events in the story occur as follows. Emily Grierson is a young southern belle who falls on hard times when her father dies in 1894. Some years later, she meets Homer Baron, a Northerner, who has come to the town of Jefferson to pave the sidewalks. They date for a period of time, and the townspeople think they will marry. Emily visits the pharmacist and buys some arsenic. Homer disappears. Some townspeople complain about a noxious odor emanating from Emily's house. The years pass. For a while, Emily teaches little girls how to paint pictures onto china. More years pass, and Emily becomes more and more reclusive. She refuses to allow the town authorities to attach a number to her house to help the postman deliver mail. She refuses to pay taxes. By now in her seventies, she dispatches a group of town councilors who come to her house to collect her back taxes. She tells them to talk to Colonel Sartoris, the mayor of Jefferson, and he will explain everything to them. Sartoris was the mayor before Emily even knew Homer and is long-since dead. Finally, at the age of seventy-four, Emily dies. Townspeople find the remains of Homer's body in her bedroom. A strand of gray hair on the pillow indicates that Emily continued to lie with Homer long after she poisoned him.

Faulkner deliberately alters the chronological order of the events in the story. He begins by telling of the death of Emily, then flashes way back to 1894 when Mayor Sartoris remitted the Grierson taxes. Then he moves forward, describing the visit from the aldermen. Next, he describes the complaint about the smell, then he flashes way back again to describe the death of Emily's father. He then moves forward again to describe the courtship of Emily and Homer, Emily's purchase of the arsenic, and the disappearance of Homer. The story comes full circle as the author again describes Emily's death. It ends with the discovery of Homer's body and the evidence of Emily's necrophilia.

Faulkner narrates his story out of chronological order for two reasons. First, the technique increases the suspense in what is, in a sense, a murder mystery. Second, the lack of chronological sequence reflects the main character's insanity—her own inability to cope with, even understand, the passing of time.

Andre Dubus, The Curse

Dubus's story also derives much of its power from its non-sequential plot. It opens in a bar the police have just left, with the main character, Mitch, feeling exhausted. Immediately the reader senses something significant has happened and wants to know what. Here the story moves back in time to the arrival of a gang of bikers who invade the bar where Mitch works. It is just about closing time. A young girl walks in to buy cigarettes and is raped by the bikers. Mitch is powerless to prevent the crime. The bikers leave and he calls the police and the bar manager. An ambulance takes the girl to the hospital.

Mitch returns home, tells his story, and is comforted by his wife. Next morning he tells the story to his stepchildren. Later the same day, back at the bar, he tells the story to his customers. He feels guilty about doing nothing to prevent the attack, but everyone—his family, friends, and customers—insist that he did exactly the right thing.

The story ends with another dramatic flashback, as Mitch sees the bikers raping the young girl and agonizes over his inability to prevent the violence. By returning, in this way, to the beginning of the story at the end of the story, Dubus intensifies the appalling dilemma of a man who knows he could have done nothing to prevent the rape—indeed he would have been beaten up himself had he tried—yet who cannot escape the possibility of his own cowardice.

Carolyn Kizer, Bitch

Kizer's poem is an example of a narrative that proceeds chronologically, flashes back to an earlier, happier time, then proceeds to its conclusion. By chance, the narrator meets an old love on the street. She is polite to him, asks about his children nonchalantly, even though she clearly still has feelings for him. Her mind flashes back to the time they were together, how she loved him and lived for the occasional kind word or gesture she received from him. She returns to the present encounter and manages to say "Give my regards to your wife" (line 32), even though she very nearly chokes on the words, and she bids him goodbye.

The nonsequentiality of the poem's plot helps carry the theme of the agony of suppressed feelings. The initial encounter is superficially polite, but all the while, the bitch inside the narrator growls and "starts to bark hysterically" (line 6), as she recalls past injustices. The bitch settles as she remembers the good times, but rears up again as she compares herself to "the well-groomed pets of his new friends" (line 31). But the narrator does not let the bitch off the leash, as perhaps she should, and ends the encounter frustrated, her pent-up emotions left unexpressed.

Stephen Dixon, All Gone

"All Gone" is an example of a story with a basically sequential plot, interrupted by one key episode, which is narrated after its chronological occurrence. The story is set in New York.

Maria, the young woman who narrates the story, gets worried when her boyfriend does not answer his phone. She calls his landlord, from whom she learns her boyfriend, Eliot, never made it home from a morning visit to the narrator's apartment. She calls the police and learns that Eliot died after being thrown onto the subway tracks. Eliot's body is flown to his mother in Seattle for the funeral, which Maria cannot attend because she cannot afford the airfare. Instead, she organizes a brief memorial service, which Eliot's friends and co-workers attend.

It is at this point, after the service, that the narrator flashes back to describe the circumstances of Eliot's death, which an elderly witness has communicated to the police. Apparently Eliot intervened to help a young woman who was being threatened by a man. This man and his friend assault Eliot and throw him onto the tracks. His head hit the tracks and he was killed.

Here the story returns to the present. Maria becomes obsessed with capturing her boyfriend's killers. She spends her Saturdays at the subway station where the tragedy occurred, waiting for the two young men, whose descriptions she has, to reappear, whereupon she will summon a police officer and have them arrested. Months go by without success. A man named Vaughn, who has noticed her spending Saturday after Saturday sitting in the station, tries to befriend her, but she brushes him off. He persists and Maria begins to become interested in him but then he stops coming to her station. She, too, stops spending her Saturdays in the subway, after she decides to give up her search for Eliot's killers. She runs into Vaughn again in a grocery store parking lot but he no longer appears interested in striking up a friendship. Several weeks later, she learns from the newspaper that the two young men have been caught. She follows the story of their trial. Unfortunately, the elderly witness has died, the girl cannot be found, and the killers get off with a light sentence.

"All Gone" is about the effect of violence on the victim's loved ones. Maria closes herself off from human contact after Eliot's death. She becomes instantly suspicious of anyone who expresses an interest in becoming close to her. As a result, she misses the chance to establish a friendship with someone whom she spurns because she thinks he will do her harm. By the time she realizes Vaughn is not only harmless but attractive, he has lost interest. The story's title refers to Maria's opportunity for happiness, robbed from her in a New York subway station.

THE ARCHETYPAL PLOT

An **archetypal plot** is a sequence of events forming a type of story that has recurred throughout the history of a civilization and that is, consequently, shared by all members of that civilization. The psychologist Carl Jung argued that an archetype is part of our subconscious heritage, and that we share such stories on a subconscious level. The battle between good and evil is an example of an archetypal plot that runs through our culture from Homer through Milton to *Star Wars.* The quest is another example of an archetypal plot manifested in such stories as Jason and the Argonauts' quest for the golden fleece and the many stories whose plots revolve around the search for the Holy Grail, the communal cup Christ used at the Last Supper.

Joseph Conrad, Heart of Darkness

The rescue is another example of an archetypal plot. Typically, the rescue archetype involves a hero overcoming a villain to rescue a damsel in distress. Joseph Conrad's novella *Heart of Darkness* is also an example of the rescue archetype, but under a different set of circumstances. It is the story of an unemployed English sailor, Charlie Marlow, who is commissioned by a major trading company to sail into the heart of Africa and bring home one of the company's agents, Kurtz. At one time, Kurtz had been a most successful ivory merchant; however, something has happened to him, and the company, desperate to protect its economic interests, needs to find out what. Marlow endures punishing journeys at sea and on land. His patience is tested when he must wait for months for his steamer to be repaired. He witnesses the inhuman treatment of the African people who are no more than slaves for European companies exploiting Africa's riches, its ivory specifically.

Finally, he reaches Kurtz. Kurtz had come to Africa, not only to strike it rich but also as a humanitarian determined to improve conditions among the exploited African people. But he, too, is corrupted by the chance for immense wealth and power. He harvests all of the ivory he can find, and ultimately establishes himself as the leader of the African people among whom he lives. He is emotionally, mentally, and physically exhausted when Marlow manages finally to rescue him (against his will) and sneak him onboard. He dies onboard, but not before he realizes what he has become, not before he repents—with the much-quoted line, "The horror, the horror"—the loss of his humanity, which has been corrupted by the greed and exploitation that characterize European imperialism.

Heart of Darkness is an archetypal rescue story (see Chapter 14). It is also Conrad's indictment against European imperialism. It is also a quest and includes, even, the descent into the underworld, which is an archetypal element of the quest legend. Marlow's journey to the heart of the dark continent is his own symbolic journey to enlightenment. He is, in fact, compared to Buddha (who achieved enlightenment through suffering) several times throughout the story. Through his contact with the ivory traders, he learns the truth about the European mission in Africa. The adjectives "civilized" to describe Europe and "uncivilized" to describe Africa are used, ironically, several times throughout the story. Through his contact with Kurtz, he learns that power can corrupt even good men; that, given a certain set of circumstances, especially the opportunity for enormous wealth and power, we might forget about our values and ideals.

It is significant that Marlow tells his tale to a lawyer, an accountant, and a company director. They represent the Establishment, and, as such, are the very men who need to learn the lessons Marlow learned through his literal and psychological descent into the heart of darkness.

Robert Frost, Directive

The quest for the Holy Grail, as a symbol of spiritual enlightenment, is a common archetypal literary plot. The famous adventures of King Arthur and the Knights of the Round Table, for example, revolve around the quest for the Holy Grail, the chalice Christ used at the Last Supper. Thomas Mallory's *Mort d'Arthur,* T. S. Eliot's *The Waste Land,* and Alfred, Lord Tennyson's *Idylls of the King* are among the many well-known works that deal with this quest legend.

"Directive" is framed as a story about the narrator's nostalgic return to a home now destroyed and abandoned. But there are hints throughout the narrative that the journey is metaphorical and is really a search for spiritual solace. When the narrator writes of getting lost on his journey, we sense he is lost as much in the spiritual as in the literal sense:

> And if you're lost enough to find yourself
> By now, pull in your ladder road behind you
> And put a sign up CLOSED to all but me.
> (lines 36–38)

As this sixty-two-line blank-verse poem nears an end, the narrator mentions the Grail specifically, and alludes to the claim in the Gospel of St. Mark (16.16) that those who are not baptized cannot be saved.

"Directive" is, then, an example of a narrative poem that has an archetypal plot beneath a surface plot that is typically sequential.

THE PLOT TWIST

Readers do not like predictable plots, so writers will often twist their plot away from the direction in which it appears to be heading. A character will die unexpectedly or a secret will be revealed or a will will be discovered or an innocent-looking character will be revealed as the guilty party, and, as a result, the plot will strike out in a whole new direction.

James Thurber, The Catbird Seat

In "The Catbird Seat" a mild-mannered file clerk, Mr. Martin, resolves to murder a supervisor, Mrs. Ulgine Barrows, who is threatening to restructure his precious department. Late one night he shows up at the supervisor's flat, determined to do her in. But as he converses with his victim, a whole new idea begins to blossom and the plot of the story twists away from the direction in which it seemed to be heading.

To Mrs. Barrows' utter amazement, Mr. Martin, who is famous at work for his abstemious habits and modest lifestyle, accepts a drink and a smoke. Then, to Mrs. Barrows' continued amazement, he refers to their boss, Mr. Fitweiler, as a "windbag" and "an old goat" and claims he is going to murder him when he is "coked to the gills" on heroin. Next day, Mrs. Barrows reports the incident to Mr. Fitweiler. Fitweiler calls Martin in and asks him if he visited Mrs. Barrows last night and made all kinds of threats. Martin appears stunned and denies everything. Mr. Fitweiler sends for the men in white coats who haul Mrs. Barrows, kicking and screaming, away, while Martin returns to his beloved files, "wearing a look of studious concentration."

Elizabeth Bishop, The Fish

"The Fish" is an example of a narrative free-verse poem that ends with a plot twist. As the story begins, the narrator catches a "tremendous fish" (line 1), which put up no fight, despite its size. She describes the fish as old, homely, and sullen. Then her attention turns to the fish's lower lip from which hangs five now ingrown old fishhooks. As she stares in amazement at this sight, she marvels at the strength and courage the old fish must have had once, "and victory filled up/the little rented boat" (lines 66–67). She stares at the rainbow of oil around the rusty engine, "until everything/was rainbow, rainbow, rainbow!" (lines 74–75). The narrator lets the fish go.

What starts out, then, as a fish story turns out to be a comment on the nature of beauty and on the value of courage and tenacity. The narrator knows the fish deserves a natural death, having lived so determined a life.

PLOT AND IRONY

Irony is the distance between what is supposed to happen and what really does happen. It is ironic when the Chief of Police is convicted of a crime, when the heart specialist has a heart attack, or when a professional writer makes a spelling error. In literature, drama especially, irony (known as **dramatic irony**) can exert a powerful influence on plot. The audience at a play squirms when a character says something he or she believes to be true but the audience knows to be false. Shakespeare's Othello, for example, is always praising Iago for his loyalty. The audience knows Iago is systematically plotting Othello's downfall behind Othello's back. The irony of Othello's praise intensifies the audience's interest in the plot's development and outcome.

Thomas Hardy, The Ruined Maid

In his poem "The Ruined Maid" Thomas Hardy uses irony to defuse the myth of the superiority of the simple country life over the wicked temptations of the city. A young farm worker, on a visit to the city, sees an old friend. The farm girl had been told that this friend, Amelia, had succumbed to the temptations of the city, been forced into prostitution, and was now a broken, "ruined maid." Amelia, however, is nothing of the kind. In fact, she is beautifully dressed, the picture of health, well-spoken, and content. Her responses to her friend's questions resonate with irony. When the farm girl comments on Amelia's improved speech, Amelia comments, "Some polish is gained with one's ruin" (line 12). The ultimate irony comes, in the last stanza of Hardy's six-stanza poem, when the farm girl expresses her wish to be just like her old friend. Note the anapestic rhythm (see Chapter 2) of the lines:

> "I wish I had feathers, a fine sweeping gown,
> And a delicate face, and could strut about Town!"
> "My dear—a raw country girl, such as you be,
> Cannot quite expect that. You ain't ruined," said she.
> (lines 21–24).

Laurie Colwin, An Old-Fashioned Story

"The Rodkers had a son named Nelson. . . . The Leopolds had a daughter named Elizabeth." So begins Colwin's "An Old-Fashioned Story," a beginning that, in combination with the title, suggests an eventual romantic liaison between Nelson and Elizabeth.

The complicating factor is that Elizabeth, a natural-born rebel, hates Nelson, "a model child in every way." Their parents' friendship forces them to spend time together, but Elizabeth hates every minute of it. She is attracted, instead, to Nelson's brother James, a rebel like herself, a young man who gets expelled from every expensive prep school his parents send him to and who ends up in Europe living a Bohemian life. As the years go by and Elizabeth graduates from college and begins work in publishing, she continues to see Nelson to whom she begins to warm, regarding him as "an excellent time filler." She secretly admires his success, which he has managed to combine with a strong social conscience.

Eventually, James returns from Europe and, at the Rodkers' Christmas party, Elizabeth finally has the chance to seduce him. But she finds him dull and self-centered and the fling she had waited for all her life fizzles. A few weeks later, Nelson declares his love for Elizabeth, and, to her own amazement, Elizabeth realizes that she has fallen in love with him.

"An Old-Fashioned Story" is built around one of the most common ironic plots in literature, a plot found in the works of Jane Austen, William Shakespeare, Charles Dickens, and many other canonical writers: The story's main character ends up in love with someone she thought she hated. This character sees something in another that is missing but needed in herself, and hates the other, subconsciously, for having what she needs. But by the end of the story, the main character has matured enough to recognize that her apparent antagonist has this quality she needs but lacks. With this recognition comes the realization that the main character's apparent antagonist is actually her soul mate. Such stories typically end with the two characters declaring their love for each other and planning a future together.

Maxine Kumin, Woodchucks

The irony of Kumin's poem "Woodchucks" is that, in the course of her narrative, a nature-loving pacifist arms herself and begins to kill off a family of woodchucks that is raiding her garden.

The story begins with a description of a failed attempt to eliminate the woodchucks by gassing them. The next morning they are back, raiding the vegetable path. The narrator picks up her .22 and opens fire, proudly killing the mother woodchuck and her babies. "The murderer inside me rose up hard," she writes, "the hawkeye killer came on stage forthwith" (lines 23–24). She becomes a hunter and clearly enjoys the power and control her .22 gives her.

As the poem comes to an end, she is beginning to reflect upon what has happened to her. She begins to see how we can change, how our values and ideals can be challenged when we are the victims even of imagined injustice. "If only they'd consented to die unseen," she concludes, "gassed underground the quiet Nazi way" (lines 29–30). She understands how ordinary people can be capable of monstrous acts of evil when they imagine that they are really only protecting themselves.

Note, as well, this poem's predominantly iambic pentameter rhythm, its unique rhyme scheme, and its exceptional use of half rhyme (see Chapter 2).

William Shakespeare, Othello

In a play, irony, usually called **dramatic irony,** occurs when a character believes something that the audience knows to be a lie. In Shakespeare's *Othello,* for example, Iago manipulates Othello into believing that his wife, Desdemona, is cheating on him. Iago is furious because Othello, a general in the Venetian army, made Lieutenant Cassio his second-in-command, a position Iago coveted and expected to get. To avenge himself, Iago masterminds Cassio's dismissal by getting him drunk and starting a brawl, and by craftily managing to make the whole fiasco appear to be Cassio's fault. Othello does, indeed, dismiss Cassio, and he then makes Iago his right-hand man.

Still, Iago covets vengeance. He continues to despise Cassio, even though he now has Cassio's job. He convinces Othello that Cassio is having an affair with his wife, Desdemona. He steals one of Desdemona's handkerchiefs and plants it on Cassio's mistress so that it appears as if Cassio has stolen the handkerchief from one lover, Desdemona, and given it as a gift to another. Othello is duped, and, blinded by fury, and convinced he is doing what he must do, he murders his wife. Eventually, Iago's wife Emilia reveals her husband's treachery and Othello, overcome by grief, commits suicide.

The dramatic irony is that Othello is convinced that Iago is honest and always has his General's best interests at heart. Othello trusts in the loyalty that Iago constantly, though hypocritically, affirms. After Cassio is dismissed, for example, he innocently pleads his case to Desdemona who promises to do what she can to persuade her husband to forgive Cassio. Iago and Othello arrive on the scene just as Cassio is leaving Desdemona, and immediately Iago plants the seeds of jealousy in Othello's mind. Desdemona then pleads Cassio's case eloquently before her husband, and, when she leaves, Iago uses all of his manipulative skills to make Othello suspicious about Desdemona's motives. Othello actually thanks Iago for his concern. Iago replies: "Trust me! . . . / I hope you will consider what is spoke / Comes from my love" (3.3. 215–217). The irony of Iago's words are overpowering to the audience, aware of Iago's duplicity.

Desdemona provides another example of dramatic irony after she loses the handkerchief that will eventually provide Iago with the "ocular proof," which Othello demands, of Desdemona's infidelity. Desdemona is dismayed over losing her handkerchief but heartened by her belief that Othello will not condemn her for it because, as she tells Emilia, "my noble Moor / Is true of mind and made of no such baseness / As jealous creatures are" (3.4. 26–28). Ironically, the audience has already witnessed Othello driven nearly mad with jealousy over his wife's apparent relationship with Cassio.

The irony Desdemona invokes becomes even stronger, indeed almost oppressive, later in the play after Othello confronts Desdemona with what he believes to be her betrayal. In despair, Desdemona turns to, of all people, Iago, and asks him for his help and advice. "Good friend," she says to him, "go to him; for, by this light of heaven, / I know not how I lost him" (4.2. 150–151).

The audience, in on Iago's treachery from the start, recognizes the irony of the trust others place in him. We recognize Iago's habit of saying one thing and doing another, of pretending to be a friend but turning out to be a mortal enemy, of going to any extreme to get what he wants. In *Othello* irony propels the plot. Right up until the end, the main characters act as they do because they trust the very man who is out to destroy them.

Character

Readers naturally respond to the characters in literature on a more familiar level than they respond to other literary elements. Readers tend to **identify** with a fictitious character, comparing the character's values, ideals, actions, goals, appearance, and personality with their own. This identification adds interest to the plot of the story (the subject of Chapter 4) and depth to the theme (see Chapter 8). A character might change as a result of the experience he or she undergoes throughout the story or miss the opportunity to change. A character who does change as a result of experience is known as a **dynamic** or a **round** character; a character who does not is known as a **static** or a **flat** character. A **stereotypical** character is a person identified by one dominant trait, such as vanity, sloth, or greed. A character's actions can illustrate the **irony** of life. A writer can poke fun at or **satirize** society through the actions of his or her characters.

DYNAMIC CHARACTERS

A **dynamic** character, sometimes referred to as a **round** character, is one whose values, attitudes, and/or ideals change as a result of the experience the character undergoes throughout the story. In Chapter 1, we met Napoleon, the main character of Frank O'Connor's story "Guests of the Nation" and noted how the execution of two British soldiers changed his perception of the war. In Chapter 4, we met Laura Sheridan whose attitude towards the social structure of her community changes as a result of her brief experience with the family of the dead carter. Napoleon and Laura are examples of dynamic characters.

D. H. Lawrence, The Odor of Chrysanthemums

Elizabeth Bates, the main character in D. H. Lawrence's story "The Odor of Chrysanthemums," changes as a result of a tragic experience around which the story's plot revolves. Elizabeth is an educated and intelligent woman married to a Nottingham miner and bitter because her marriage is not working out. She is exasperated by her humble lifestyle and constantly angry at her hard-drinking husband. On the night the story is set, her husband is late yet again for dinner, and Elizabeth thinks he has gone to the pub. But as the evening advances and he still does not return, she begins to worry.

The odor of chrysanthemums has always been associated with a significant event in Elizabeth's life. Elizabeth's daughter Annie loves the chrysanthemums Elizabeth has in the pocket of her apron and tells her mother how beautiful they are. Elizabeth replies they are not beautiful to her because she associates them with her marriage, the birth of her children, and the first time Walter was brought home drunk, because he had a chrysanthemum in his buttonhole. Annie's reference to the flowers foreshadows a significant event to come.

Elizabeth asks her neighbor if he can discover the whereabouts of her husband. Soon she learns there has been an accident at the mine and Walter has suffocated. There is some evidence to suggest the "accident" was, in fact, a suicide. The doctor notes that Walter's body was not crushed; the mine manager says "seems as if it was done on purpose."

Consciously, Elizabeth does not respond to this possibility, but subconsciously, as she cleans her husband's body, she begins to realize she was not the only one unhappy in the marriage, that Walter's guilt over his inability to make her happy might have contributed to his drinking and possibly to the "accident" as well. Elizabeth moves beyond herself and her own disappointment and begins to see their life together from her late husband's point of view. She realizes, with shame, that she "had denied him as himself." She failed to accept her husband for what he was, he sensed her disappointment, and was, himself, unhappy.

Lawrence wrote that he believed marriage should be a "mutual unison in separateness." The insight that makes Elizabeth so dynamic a character is her realization that, consumed as she was by her own bitterness and disappointment, she failed to acknowledge her husband's despair over his inability to make her happy. She failed to give him a chance; she failed to acknowledge his own separateness.

Herman Melville, Bartleby, the Scrivener

The narrator of Melville's story "Bartleby, the Scrivener" is another example of a dynamic character. His change is remarkable because he is a conservative Wall Street lawyer whose life has been, by choice, conventional, staid, and uneventful. He is prosperous, a bachelor, solitary, and set in his ways.

His change is precipitated by a scrivener, or legal secretary, who walks into his office in response to the narrator's classified ad. He begins work and is, at first, a hard-working, exemplary employee. However, as time passes, and for no apparent reason, Bartleby begins to deny his employer's requests, saying simply, "I prefer not to." He stays behind his office partition, copying, but refusing to do anything else. He spends time staring out of his window at a brick wall. Eventually, the narrator discovers that Bartleby is living in his office. Soon, Bartleby refuses even to do his copying, the main task of a scrivener.

Finally, the narrator has no choice but to fire Bartleby, but Bartleby "prefers not" to budge. The narrator's professional friends begin to wonder about the pale apparition who haunts their colleague's office. Bartleby is beginning to be bad for business. The narrator moves to different offices, to escape from his eccentric scrivener. But the tenants who take over his old office insist he is responsible for the strange man who now haunts the hallways and who refuses to leave. The narrator tries once more to reason with Bartleby but to no avail. At last, Bartleby is arrested as a vagrant and imprisoned. In prison, Bartleby stares at the walls, stops eating, and eventually lies down and dies.

The narrator is a man who has never before been faced with the responsibility of caring for someone else. He has controlled his life in a way that has made him responsible for no one but himself. He has walled himself in, a metaphor reinforced by the walls that surround him, the many walls Bartleby stares at forlornly, the very location, Wall Street, where he conducts his business. Bartleby forces him to realize he is a part of a larger community and that, try as he might, he cannot wall himself in. He must be a participant in his society, not only as a lawyer but as a human being, too. He has to help others on a human as well as on a business level. At the end of the story, responding to Bartleby's death and the effect it has on his values and ideals, the narrator says much with few words when he writes simply: "Ah Bartleby! Ah humanity!"

Sherwood Anderson, I'm a Fool

The narrator and main character of Anderson's story is a dynamic character with a vengeance. Indeed, he says as much in the story's opening sentences, which are virtually the mantra of the dynamic character: "It was a hard jolt for me, one of the most bitterest I have had to face. And it all came about through my own foolishness, too." The foolishness of which the narrator speaks is universal: He lies to impress a girl.

The narrator is a young man of humble origins, by profession a swipe, one who grooms and cares for racehorses. On a day off, he attends the races where he meets a young woman who is obviously of a higher social class than he. They are attracted to each other and, fortified by a few drinks our narrator has before the races, he tells Lucy that his father owns one of the horses and that they kept stables in their grand house "on a hill, up above the Ohio River."

His problem is that he is genuinely attracted to Lucy as she is to him, and they want to continue to see each other. She must return home but she promises to write so they can eventually get together again. But he has given her a false name and made up his life story. Her letters will never reach him. If he tells her the truth, she will know he is a liar and think him unstable and will not likely want to see him again. As Lucy's train pulls out of the station, the narrator is furious with himself and in agony over an opportunity lost because of his vanity and pride.

The change in this narrator's character, then, is dramatic. In losing Lucy, he learns all about the hazards of claiming to be something you are not and about the importance of simply being yourself.

STATIC CHARACTERS

A static character, also known as a **flat** character, is one who is offered the chance for positive change but who, for one reason or another, fails to embrace it. The character might be too afraid to change. He or she might be naïve and not realize there is a need to change. The character might be too proud to change in a way that might inconvenience him or her, even while it might benefit someone else.

T. S. Eliot, The Love Song of J. Alfred Prufrock

T. S. Eliot's J. Alfred Prufrock is a typical static character. He doesn't like who he is, and he wants to change. He is a middle-aged man who would like to have a serious relationship with a woman but who is too insecure to ask the woman the "overwhelming question," which would lead to such a relationship.

Throughout his dramatic monologue, Prufrock speculates on the kind of man he would like to be. He would like to be a romantic figure like Michaelangelo whom women talk about. He would like to be heroic, like John the Baptist, miraculous like Lazarus, or the leader that Hamlet finally becomes. He would like to ask the woman to marry him, perhaps, or perhaps simply to like and respect him enough to at least consider a more serious relationship. But he is obsessed with his bald head and skinny arms; worried that his clothes are not right; convinced he lacks a winning personality. His most pronounced concern is a fear of rejection, a fear that if he bears his soul to this woman, she will proclaim her lack of interest, thereby completely shattering his already fragile self-esteem. And so he does nothing. He expresses his desire to change his image, dress more stylishly, assert himself more, but he is stuck in his conservative middle-aged rut.

And so the poem ends as it began. Prufrock is convinced the mermaids will not sing for him. He is, metaphorically, drowned by his inability to relate to others the way he would like to. He is static, and he seems incapable of becoming the man he would like to be.

Katherine Mansfield, Her First Ball

Leila, the main character of Mansfield's story "Her First Ball," is offered a chance to learn a lesson about the transience of life, but she turns her back on the opportunity, choosing instead to remain with the romantic vision she prefers to the reality she is not ready to accept.

Leila is a young woman attending her first formal ball. She is overwhelmed by excitement, which increases as she glides around the floor with attractive young men. Then she dances with a much older, much less attractive man who nearly spoils the party for her. Pointing to the mothers and grandmothers watching the dancing from the stage, the old man tells Leila that before she knows it, she will be one of them, her youthful beauty will fade, and she will have only memories of her youth to share with other middle-aged women. For a moment, Leila senses some truth in the old man's words, and, for a moment, she is confused and downhearted. But as soon as another handsome young man asks her to dance, she puts the old man's words out of her mind. Indeed, when her next partner bumps into the old man, she smiles defiantly, refusing to recognize him or his admonition to her.

Leila is, then, the same starry-eyed young girl at the end of the story that she was at the beginning. She is static, unwilling to accept the old man's warning. Her defiance is a victory in the sense that she has decided to live for the moment and enjoy the happiness and pleasure of her first ball. Her victory is tarnished by her refusal, at the end, even to acknowledge an old man's wisdom.

STEREOTYPICAL CHARACTERS

A **stereotypical** character is one who can be identified by a single dominant trait. In our discussion of comedy in Chapter 3, we noted that stereotypical characters are often sources of humor, though it is a humor sometimes tinged with racism and sexism in stereotypes such as the blond bimbo or the parsimonious Scot. Stereotypes are also associated with various professions: The absent-minded professor, the scruffy artist, the dumb jock are all stereotypical characters.

Stereotypical characters are not necessarily one-dimensional. They can be identified by a single dominant trait, but that trait does not necessarily compose the whole of their personality. They can be complex and well-rounded characters.

Robert Browning, My Last Duchess

The Duke of Ferrar, the narrator of Robert Browning's classic poem "My Last Duchess," is a stereotypical control freak. In his dramatic monologue, he addresses an ambassador from the court of the Count of Tyrol, whose daughter he wants to marry. The duke shows off a portrait of his former wife, his last duchess, and, in the process, tells the ambassador about her. He has an ulterior motive in doing so. He does not want the count's daughter to make the same mistakes his last duchess made and meet the same fate she met.

The duke comes across as a man obsessed with his own self-importance, a man who insists his social inferiors, among whom he includes his wife, pay due deference to him and his "nine-hundred-years-old name" (line 33). His last duchess, it appears, was not sufficiently in awe of him. She flirts with other men and treats her husband like an ordinary man. He refuses to talk to his wife and explain his concerns to her because he feels it would be a sign of weakness, "and I choose / Never to stoop" (lines 42–43). And so he has her murdered:

> . . . I gave commands;
> Then all smiles stopped together . . .
> (lines 45–46)

He tells all this to the count's ambassador so that the count's
daughter will know the proper way to behave in so august a
presence.

The duke is vain and arrogant. He insists people beneath
him act the way he expects them to act. If they do not, they
are disposed of unceremoniously. Like many stereotypical
characters, however, his dominant trait might mask an even
stronger trait that lurks beneath his overt personality. Many
readers sense some fear and insecurity beneath the duke's
arrogance and vanity.

F. Scott Fitzgerald, The Great Gatsby

Jay Gatsby, the title character of Fitzgerald's novel, is the
stereotypical American dreamer. He thinks that if he can get
the money and get the dream girl, he can live happily ever
after. He is the poor boy who recognizes that through hard
work and a winning personality he can, in a country like
America, transcend his social class, get rich, and win the
hand of the princess.

Gatsby first meets Daisy when he is a young lieutenant,
stationed in her Kentucky town, before he is sent to Europe
to fight in the First World War. After the war, he spends a
few months at Oxford before he returns to America. By this
time, Daisy has married Tom Buchanan, but Gatsby refuses
to acknowledge the fact that Daisy is not available and is determined to win her back. To do so, he reasons, he must get
rich, which he does—this being the period of prohibition—
selling bootleg whiskey. He buys a mansion across the bay
from Daisy's house and arranges to meet her through her
cousin, Nick, who lives next door to Gatsby and who is the
story's narrator. For a time, Daisy and Gatsby actually do get
back together and carry on an affair. But Tom Buchanan,
Daisy's husband, has learned the truth about Gatsby and, in
a dramatic scene, confronts Gatsby with the truth and fright-
ens his wife into breaking off her relationship with him. On
the drive back to the Buchanan mansion, Daisy hits and kills
Myrtle Wilson, who happens to be her husband's mistress.
Myrtle recognizes the car, thinks it is Tom, and rushes into
the street to stop it. To protect Daisy, Gatsby claims it was
he who was driving the car. Myrtle's husband learns this,
stalks, and eventually murders Gatsby. The Buchanans disappear, and Nick is left to arrange Gatsby's funeral.

Nick sees in Gatsby the romantic idealist who believes
that love follows money, that with money, anything is

possible. This is, after all, America. What money can't do, though, is stop the march of time. Daisy and Gatsby are separated for five years, a period of time which Gatsby refuses to acknowledge. In the novel's central scene, Daisy and Gatsby reunite in Nick's house. Gatsby leans against the mantle and nearly knocks over an old clock, a symbolic attempt to kill time, his enemy. Later on, Gatsby is shocked when Nick tells him you can't repeat the past, angrily insisting that of course you can. So intent is he on achieving his goal, that Gatsby has suspended disbelief. Until his death, his dream is his reality. Gatsby is the stereotypical American dreamer, destroyed because he cannot recognize that money will not necessarily buy happiness.

Samuel Beckett, Krapp's Last Tape

Krapp, the only character in Beckett's brief, one-act play, is the stereotypical bitter old man. Poor and lonely, probably alcoholic, Krapp passes his time listening to his tape-recorded journal through which he relives happier times. He listens to a tape he made on his thirty-ninth birthday, on the eve of his middle age. The tape tells of the death of his mother. It tells of an even earlier tape he had been listening to, recorded when he was living with a young woman, named Bianca. But now, at thirty-nine, he has apparently decided to end his relationship with Bianca, though he clearly retains strong feelings for her. Every so often, Krapp stops the tape and walks off stage; the off-stage noise clearly indicates he is drinking.

He turns the old tape off and begins to record a new one. He begins by condemning the sentimentality he heard in the tape he had been listening to, recorded thirty years ago. Yet still he cannot get Bianca out of his mind. He speaks of his failure as a writer. He speaks of other fleeting relationships with women. He hints at a wish for a spiritual dimension to his life: He attended Vespers but was drunk and fell off the pew. As the play comes to an end, he puts on the old tape once again and listens to his lyrical description of a beautiful evening spent with Bianca.

Krapp's Last Tape presents the musing of a bitter old man who knows, though he won't admit, that he has missed his chance for happiness. He has turned away from love. He has turned away from faith. He has become bitter and cynical, pretending he does not miss the days when he was young and at least had the chance for happiness. There is nothing for him now but to wait for his own death. "Now the day is over," he sings, as the play ends, "Night is drawing nigh-igh, / Shadows . . . of the evening / Steal across the sky."

Katherine Ann Porter, The Jilting of Granny Weatherall

Granny Weatherall is the stereotypical feisty old woman who refuses to acknowledge and accept the fact that she is sick and probably dying, and thereby confess to any weakness. She is attended by a young doctor who she watched grow up and who she still thinks of as a boy in knee breeches, now playing doctor.

Granny Weatherall's strength is the product of her stereotypically hard life. Her husband died when their children were young, and she had to raise them and run a farm on her own, experiences that strengthened her determination and resolve. One child, Hapsy, died in infancy. She has, as her name suggests, weathered it all.

As she lies sick in bed musing, she relives another experience that clearly shaped her character: She was, as a young woman, jilted by her fiancé and, literally, left at the altar. Typically, she refuses to let the experience embitter her and, instead, she fights and triumphs over her wounded vanity.

At the end of the story, her children, her doctor, and her priest gather around her bed. In character to the end, she chides the priest for coming, announcing that she is "not so sinful as all that." She imagines she sees Hapsy at the end of her bed. She thinks of all the things she still has to do, the chores and the errands she must discharge, the will she needs to change.

Porter's description of Ellen Weatherall, as she slips into death, is vivid and compelling. The last light that she sees, a light from a lampshade, becomes a tiny point of light "in the center of her brain." It flickers and dwindles as she hovers between life and death. She relives the cruelty of the man who left her at the altar, as another bridegroom, life, leaves her at the altar. But, in control until the end, it is Granny Weatherall herself who draws in one last breath and blows out the light of her life.

CHARACTER AND IRONY

In our discussion of plot, in Chapter 4, we defined irony as the distance between what is supposed to happen and what actually does happen. In literature, a character's actions are ironic if that character behaves in a way that is at odds with the way that person appears to be. We expect the vicar will be righteous, so we say it is ironic when he is found in bed with the bishop's wife. Indeed, in literature, irony and hypocrisy are often bedfellows.

Edwin Arlington Robinson, Richard Cory

The title character, Richard Cory, is a man who seems to have everything going for him. He is rich, good looking, and widely respected. Ordinary people who live in his community look at Richard Cory and wish they could be like him. The irony is that, despite superficial appearances, Richard is desperately unhappy, as the ending of the poem makes clear:

> So on we worked, and waited for the light,
> And went without the meat, and cursed the bread;
> And Richard Cory, one calm summer night,
> Went home and put a bullet through his head.
> (lines 13–16)

Eudora Welty, A Worn Path

Phoenix Jackson, the main character of Welty's story, is a very old woman who walks many miles into town from her home in the country to buy medicine for her grandson who has seriously injured his throat by accidentally swallowing some lye. On the way, she encounters many obstacles, trivial to a fit young person but serious to Phoenix: logs along the path; a scarecrow that, for a moment, seems real to her; a barbed-wire fence. Clearly becoming senile, Phoenix talks to herself as she proceeds. She encounters a hunter who makes fun of her, patronizes her, and pretends to threaten her with his rifle. She is oblivious to his games and even takes from him a nickel, which he did not notice fall out of his pocket. She arrives in Natchez where she is treated condescendingly as a "charity case" and given the medicine her grandson needs. She talks the attendant at the clinic into giving her a nickel.

Phoenix Jackson is a poor, black, senile old woman who people treat with condescending kindness. The irony is that she manages to best all of them in every way. She gets money from the hunter without his knowing it. The attendant offers her a few pennies; "Five pennies is a nickel," Phoenix says without missing a beat. The biggest irony is that those who feel they are superior to her treat her as a charity case, when it is Phoenix herself, trekking into town to help her grandson, who embodies the true spirit of Christian charity. She is like her namesake, the Phoenix, the mythological Arabian bird that at the end of its life, sets fire to itself and emerges anew from its own ashes. Phoenix Jackson has more spirit, strength, courage, and resilience than the affluent young white people with whom she comes into contact.

William Shakespeare, Sonnet 144: Two Loves I Have of Comfort and Despair

The narrator of this Shakespeare sonnet finds himself on the horns of a major ironic dilemma. He suspects the two people he loves most of having an affair. More specifically, he suspects that his mistress, the "worser spirit," is trying to seduce his best friend, "the better angel." And he believes she has succeeded:

> And whether that my angel be turned fiend
> Suspect I may, yet not directly tell;
> But being both from me, both to each friend,
> I guess one angel in another's hell.
> (lines 9–12)

Both are away from him and friends with each other, so a sexual relationship between them is a distinct possibility. "In another's hell," to Shakespeare's readers, suggested a sexual liaison, "hell" being Elizabethan slang for vagina.

The ultimate irony is that the narrator will never know the truth, unless and until his mistress passes along to his friend a sexually-transmitted disease:

> Yet this shall I ne'er know, but live in doubt
> Till my bad angel fire my good one out.
> (lines 13–14)

To "fire out," in Elizabethan slang, is to pass on syphilis.

CHARACTER AND SATIRE

Satire is a literary form through which a writer pokes fun at those aspects of his society, especially those people and those social institutions, that the author thinks are corrupt and in need of change. There are two types of satire. **Horatian satire,** after the Roman poet Horace, is a relatively gentle type in which the author uses humor to make us laugh at people who are vain and hypocritical, and at social conditions that need reform. Pope's well-known mock-epic poem, *The Rape of the Lock,* is an example of Horatian satire, wherein Pope makes fun of a group of rich self-absorbed young people. **Juvenalian satire,** after the Roman poet Juvenal, uses bitter sarcasm more than humor and, indeed, is often tinged with cruelty. Pope's friend, Jonathan Swift, favored Juvenalian satire, evidenced by his classic work *Gulliver's Travels* wherein Swift attacks corrupt politicians and the system that sanctions dishonesty.

George Bernard Shaw, Pygmalion

One of the great satirists of the twentieth century is the playwright George Bernard Shaw. Shaw was an ardent social reformer and he often used satire as a way of alerting his audience to the injustice within their society in the hope that they might begin to effect some changes.

Through the character of Eliza Doolittle in *Pygmalion,* Shaw satirizes the class system. Eliza is a cockney flower girl, a young woman whose speech reveals her humble social status. Her Pygmalion (the title refers to a Greek sculptor who fell in love with his own statue of Galatea) is Henry Higgins, a gentleman and a phonetician who resolves to raise Eliza's social status simply by improving her speech. He does so, but in the process reveals his own arrogance and insensitivity, which is in stark contrasts to Eliza's simple good sense and compassion. Social class, Shaw implies, has a lot to do with proper speech; but genuine class has more to do with whether or not people treat each other with respect.

Shaw also satirizes, in the figures of Eliza and Higgins, the conventions of romantic comedy. The audience expects Eliza and Higgins will fall in love and marry but this Shaw resolutely avoids. At the end of the play, Eliza has left Higgins to marry the simple but devoted young gentleman Freddy Hill.

Alice Walker, Everyday Use

In "Everyday Use," Alice Walker satirizes young African Americans who seek to authenticate themselves by reclaiming their heritage, but who do so by embracing the superficial trappings of a culture they have never known, while ignoring a past in which they can genuinely take pride.

Dee Johnson, a successful, college-educated young woman, comes to visit her poor mother and sister in their modest southern home. She greets them with Black Muslim expressions. She is no longer Dee, she announces, but Wangero Leewanika Kemanjo; she has changed her name because she could no longer bear "being named after the people who oppress me." Dee's mother, who narrates the story, informs her daughter that she was in fact named after her Aunt Dicie. Dee is accompanied by one Hakim-a-barber, dressed like Dee, in traditional African clothes and sporting an African hairstyle.

Dee expresses great interest in some of the objects in her mother's house. She wants a piece of the butter churn carved by her uncle, as a centerpiece for her alcove table. Mrs. Johnson is surprised because Dee has never expressed an interest before in such objects. What she does not know is that now it is in vogue for young African Americans to have handmade objects, products of their heritage, on display in their own homes. Dee is also interested in a pair of old quilts made by her mother, her aunt, and her grandmother. But Mrs. Johnson refuses to let her take them, telling Dee they are for her sister, Maggie. Dee is shocked, claiming that Maggie will be "backward enough" to put them to everyday use. Mrs. Johnson replies she hopes so, since that is what quilts are for. Dee had planned to hang them on her walls, monuments to the pride she is taking now in her culture.

Significantly, there is a patch of cloth from Great Grandpa Ezra's Civil War uniform sewn into one of the quilts. This patch of cloth is a symbol of Dee's real heritage. For better or worse, she is not Wangero Leewanika Kemanjo, a native of Africa, but Dee Johnson, American.

Walker, an African American writer herself, in no way undermines the hostility and oppression African Americans have historically experienced from mainstream America. Rather, she satirizes young African Americans who play at being African, when they might do more for their culture by celebrating and supporting a more authentic African-American experience.

Kurt Vonnegut, Harrison Bergeron

"Harrison Bergeron" is Vonnegut's scathing satire of a society so obsessed with equality that anyone of exceptional ability in any area is deliberately handicapped by government decree. The story is set in 2081 and centers around the Bergeron family. George Bergeron is a man of superior intelligence, but because in this brave new world superior intelligence in one will make others not feel good about themselves, George is forced to wear a "mental handicap radio" in his ear, which transmits horribly distracting noises at regular intervals so that George cannot formulate a series of rational thoughts and thereby display his intelligence and make others, God forbid, feel inferior. He and his wife, Hazel, watch ballerinas weighted down with birdshot so that their dancing is merely average, not exceptional. Beautiful people are forced to wear masks so that the less beautiful will not be self-conscious about their own average looks.

But the Bergerons have a son, Harrison, who is truly exceptional in every way, so much so that he is able to overcome the obstacles the government deliberately encumbers him with, question the social order, and incite revolutionary change. He is captured and imprisoned but escapes and breaks into the nation's one television studio. Harrison defiantly pulls out the earpiece that prevents his brilliant mind from functioning properly; takes off the thick glasses, the rubber ball on his nose, and the black caps on his teeth, all of which disguise his beauty; and disposes of the three-hundred pounds of scrap metal strapped to his back, put there by government decree to diminish Harrison's super-human strength. The time has come to break the rules that force everyone to be the same. The time has come to allow talented people to realize their potential, for the betterment of all humankind.

Unfortunately, at the end of the story, the United States Handicapper General, Diana Moon Glampers, bursts into the studio and shoots to death Harrison and the beautiful ballerina he has taken as his empress. Significantly, Glampers is not hampered by any of the devices that neutralize any special talents that ordinary citizens might possess. She is a senior government official and therefore she is free. Her freedom conveys the full force of Vonnegut's satire. He is mocking and warning against a government that, by law, handicaps people ostensibly to make absolutely sure that all people are created equal and must remain equal forever. In reality, the government acts the way it does because, in this way, it can exert total control over the people. Using satire as his weapon, Vonnegut warns us against a government that paradoxically has a policy of enforced equality, not to free but to enslave its citizens in a totalitarian society.

Point of View

A story needs a storyteller. The stance from which the storyteller or **narrator** tells the story is known as the **point of view** of the story. Sometimes the narrator will be **omniscient,** that is, capable of telling readers the thoughts of all of the characters and the actions of all of the characters at any time. Sometimes the narrator will limit him- or herself to relaying to readers the thoughts and actions of the main character only; such a storyteller is known as a **limited-omniscient** narrator. The narrator will sometimes be a character in the story. A **first-person major-character narrator** tells a story in which he or she is the protagonist (see Chapter 1). From this point of view, the narrator can describe his or her thoughts but can only speculate on the thoughts of other characters. A **first-person minor-character narrator** participates in a minor way in the story but primarily observes and describes the actions of the main character and reports those to the readers. From this point of view, the narrator can only speculate on the main character's thoughts. An author will try, sometimes, to render the narrator invisible and tell the story almost exclusively through dialogue. Such a story has an **objective point of view.**

THE OMNISCIENT NARRATOR

Omniscient means "all knowing." An omniscient narrator is like a god who can provide readers with all of the information they could ever want. An omniscient narrator can tell us what all of the characters in the story are thinking and what they are doing at any time, in any place. It is a powerful point of view, especially effective in novels that contain many interesting and psychologically complex characters and sweeping action that occurs in a number of locales. Its drawbacks are that the narrator is detached, above the action rather than within it, and so it lacks the sense of realism and immediacy we get from a first-person point of view.

D. H. Lawrence, The Rocking Horse Winner

"The Rocking Horse Winner" is a good example of a story narrated from the omniscient point of view. The story delves into the minds of two characters and describes a sequence of somewhat supernatural events.

The story opens describing Hester, a beautiful woman who is embittered because she has no luck, she has not married well, and she cannot love her children. The narrator quickly moves into the mind of one of the children, Paul, who is determined to stop the voices in the house, which chant, "there must be more money!" He feels he can win his mother's love if he can solve the money problems that so divert her attention.

Paul discovers he can predict the winner of horse races by riding his rocking horse until the motion produces a trance-like effect, that culminates in a supernatural experience, during which the winner is magically revealed to him. With the help of the gardener, Bassett, and later his Uncle Oscar, Paul puts money on the races and wins a fortune. But the strain makes him seriously ill. The narrator now enters Hester's mind and reveals that she finally has developed a motherly love for Paul. Ironically, Paul dies after the strain of discovering the winner of the Derby proves to be too much for him.

The omniscient point of view is particularly well suited to "The Rocking Horse Winner" because the story is, in many ways, a **fable.** A fable is a story that often features supernatural events and characters, notably talking animals, and that contains a clear moral. The moral of this story is love is more important, especially for the health of a family, than money.

There is an interesting subtext to "The Rocking Horse Winner" as well. Some critics suggest Hester's cold heart reflects sexual unfulfillment and that, on a subconscious and Oedipal level, Paul is trying to satisfy her, the demonic rocking on his horse mirroring a form of sexual activity.

Kate Chopin, The Storm

Chopin's "The Storm" is a brief short story but, in true omniscient style, the author enters the lives, hearts, and minds of several of the characters and reports their thoughts and actions to her readers.

The story opens in a Louisiana store where a father, Bobinot, and his son, Bibi, decide to remain to wait out a threatening storm. Quickly, and typically of the omniscient point of view, the focus shifts, and readers are taken to Bobinot's home, where his wife, Calixta, is busy closing windows and doors to protect herself from the storm. By chance, an old lover of hers, Alcee, is passing by and seeks shelter. There is a passion between them still and they make love, with no apparent guilt, as the storm crashes around them.

The focus shifts back again to Bobinot and Bibi, now making their way home. Calixta greets them as the loving wife and mother she is, apparently unaffected by her passionate encounter with Alcee. Now the focus shifts to Alcee, who is writing a love letter to his wife who is holidaying with the children in Biloxi. Finally, Chopin shows us Alcee's wife, Clarisse, joyfully receiving the letter, missing her husband but enjoying some time without having to worry about the responsibilities of a southern wife.

Chopin's controversial theme is that marital infidelity is or at least can be insignificant, that it can, in fact, draw couples closer together by reminding them of their love for each other. "So the storm passed," reads Chopin's final sentence, "and everyone was happy." She needs the omniscient point of view to communicate her theme. Had she limited her point of view to the consciousness of a single person, its impact would be considerably diminished. Infidelity stories told from the first-person point of view tend to focus on guilt, and on the fear that the narrator's partner will learn of the affair and end the relationship. Chopin's point, illustrated by the ways in which Alcee and Calixta interact with their spouses in the wake of their encounter, is that infidelity might help an unfaithful spouse reaffirm his or her love for his or her partner. Chopin needs the omniscient point to express her view that infidelity can actually benefit all four people affected, and she must provide readers with access to the thoughts of all four people if she is to present her theme convincingly.

Stephen Crane, The Bride Comes to Yellow Sky

Crane narrates the first chapter of "The Bride Comes to Yellow Sky" from the limited omniscient point of view, as this passage, early in the story, makes clear:

> As a matter of truth, Jack Potter was beginning to find the shadow of a deed weigh upon him like a leaden slab. He, the town marshal of Yellow Sky, a man known, liked, and feared in his corner, a prominent person, had gone to San Antonio to meet a girl he believed he loved, and there, after the usual prayers had actually induced her to marry him, without consulting Yellow Sky for any part of the transaction.

Here, in Chapter I, Crane presents Jack Potter's thoughts, as he interacts with his bride on the train trip home.

However, in Chapter II, the scene shifts to a bar in Yellow Sky, where the patrons are taking cover because a drunk Scratchy Wilson, brandishing a pair of six-shooters, is on the rampage. Chapter III maintains the focus on Wilson, as he wanders around looking for a fight. He makes his way to Marshal Potter's house, there to challenge "his ancient antagonist." There is no one at home.

In Chapter IV, however, Crane shifts his point of view back to Marshal Potter, now making his way back to his house. In the tradition of the classic Western, Potter and Wilson meet and the stage for the showdown is set. Wilson points one of the six-shooters at the marshal's chest and threatens him. Potter is unarmed and tells this to Wilson, who becomes enraged and demands an explanation. Potter calmly tells him he is just returning to town from his wedding in San Antonio. Here the story twists away from the traditional Western: The expected gunfight at the OK Corral does not occur. Instead, the story becomes comical, as Scratchy attempts to process this bizarre information. Finally, he can only shrug and say, "I s'pose it's all off now." He goes on his way, making "funnel-shaped tracks in the heavy sand."

The omniscient point of view helps Crane achieve his goals in this story. He blends together two genres—the comic tale and the tale of the wild west—and needs to shift his point of view away from the marshal and to his comic foil, Wilson, to bring the merger to its full effect. He wants, as well, to say something on the theme of the civilizing effect of marriage, especially on men, and does so thoroughly by giving us access to the thoughts of both the good guy in the white hat, Potter, and the bad guy, in the black hat, Wilson. He could not have achieved such effects had he chosen a first-person or limited point of view.

THE LIMITED-OMNISCIENT NARRATOR

If the omniscient narrator is a god, the limited-omniscient narrator is a demigod who delves into the subconscious of only one character in the story, the protagonist. Many short stories, which tend to focus on a single character, are told from the limited-omniscient point of view.

James Joyce, Eveline

The narrator of Joyce's story "Eveline" never leaves the side of the main (the title) character. In typical limited-omniscient manner, the narrator traces Eveline's actions and tells us what she is thinking.

Eveline is a young Irish woman whose home life has been oppressive ever since the death of her mother. Her father is abusive and refuses to let her have a life of her own. When she meets a young sailor who offers to take her to Buenos Aires, she is tempted. She makes it as far as the quay, but just before boarding the ship, she has a change of heart. Her sense of obligation to her family outweighs her desire for a whole new life. Because she has been a prisoner for so long, she is suddenly afraid of what might happen to her in the outside world.

Notice, as the story nears its end, how effectively the limited-omniscient narrator communicates Eveline's inner feelings without assuming her character:

> All the seas of the world tumbled about her heart. He was drawing her into them: he would drown her. She gripped both hands at the iron railing.

Eveline's hands, gripping the iron railing, symbolize her imprisonment. As the story ends, she stares at Frank but appears not even to recognize him.

F. Scott, Fitzgerald, Babylon Revisited

Fitzgerald's "Babylon Revisited" is another example of the limited-omniscient point of view. The story is told from the point of view of Charlie Wales, an American businessman, living and working in Europe.

Charlie returns to Paris to try to regain custody of his daughter Honoria, who is in the care of his wife's sister, Marion Peters. Charlie and his wife, Helen, have been active members of that group of American expatriates living in Paris in the roaring twenties, the jazz age of Fitzgerald's own early adulthood. With a stock market out of control and easy money so readily available, Charlie's gang spend their nights partying in Paris bistros and their days sleeping off hangovers. The life becomes too much for Charlie's wife and she dies of heart failure. Charlie himself becomes an alcoholic and must dry out in a Paris sanitarium. He consents, then, to turn over custody of his daughter to his sister-in-law. The crash wipes him out and brings down the walls of the Babylon that Paris had become. Nearly a year passes, he is sober, he is successful again, and he wants Honoria back. Marion is hostile to him but her husband Lincoln is more reasonable, and eventually she agrees to let Honoria return with Charlie to Prague, where he is now working. But ghosts from Charlie's past appear in the Peters' apartment just when final plans are being made. Two old friends who refuse to admit that the party is over arrive drunk and acting as immaturely as Charlie and his wife had acted in the past. Their behavior reminds Marion of the tragedy of her sister's death, of the lifestyle she blames for that death and she reverses her decision, denying Charlie that which now he wants most in his life.

The limited-omniscient point of view effectively captures the main character's agony about his past, his ecstasy over the prospect of getting back his daughter, and his return to a sense of desperate loneliness when his past catches up with him and that which he wants the most is taken away from him again. When he sees Honoria again, after almost a year's absence:

> A great wave of protectiveness went over him. He thought he knew what to do for her. He believed in character; he wanted to jump back a whole generation and trust in character again as the eternally valuable element.

Again Fitzgerald gives us insight into Charlie's mind when he is being interrogated by Marion, whose hostility is palpable:

> Charlie became increasingly alarmed at leaving Honoria in this atmosphere of hostility against himself; sooner or later it would come out, in a word here, a shake of the head there, and some of that distrust would be irrevocably implanted in Honoria.

The end of the story gives another vivid example of Fitzgerald's mastery of the limited-omniscient viewpoint, as Charlie reflects on what he has lost, on the price he must pay for a disreputable past:

> But he wanted his child back, and nothing was much good now, beside that fact. He wasn't young anymore, with a lot of nice thoughts and dreams to have by himself. He was absolutely sure Helen wouldn't have wanted him to be so alone.

THE FIRST-PERSON MAJOR-CHARACTER NARRATOR

The first-person major-character narrator is something of an egotist. This narrator tells a story in which he or she is the main character, the focus of attention. The first-person major-character point of view, like its poetic cousin, the dramatic monologue (see Chapter 2), is especially effective for revealing the inner thoughts and the personality of a single main character.

Margaret Atwood, Rape Fantasies

Estelle, the first-person narrator of Margaret Atwood's story "Rape Fantasies," begins by describing her co-workers, as they respond to a magazine article about rape fantasies, by sharing their own. Estelle is witty and sardonic, and, with a well-chosen phrase or two, she cleverly reveals the essence of her friends' personalities.

As the story continues, however, the humor begins to fade, as Estelle tells us about her own rape fantasies. She has had many, and, in nearly all of them, she ends up befriending her would-be rapist with whom she shares something significant, such as a serious illness. In the process, Estelle reveals her true nature. She is a lonely and rather sad young woman who would like to have a serious relationship, but seems unable, except in her fantasy life, to relate to others in any intimate way. Her mordant wit, so entertaining at times, clouds her judgment of others and perhaps scares them away.

The first-person point of view reveals Estelle's personality in a way an omniscient narrator could not. An omniscient narrator would not use Estelle's own unique speech patterns and colloquial writing style, which so suit her personality and give us insight into her character. By becoming Estelle, Atwood paints a particularly vivid picture of a unique and interesting character.

Alice Munro, Boys and Girls

"Boys and Girls" is a **coming-of-age** story, which means it chronicles the main character's transition from childhood to adulthood by focusing on the life experience or experiences that precipitated the change and on the protagonist's realization that a change has occurred. Coming-of-age stories are usually told from the first-person point of view, because defining experiences, which engender significant change, are usually personal and profound.

"My father was a fox farmer." Here, in the opening sentence of her story, Munro establishes her first-person point of view. She, or rather, her first-person narrator, goes on to describe her pleasure in helping her father with his chores around the farm. She would rather be with him feeding the foxes and helping him skin them than with her mother in the kitchen, making jam and canning vegetables. Her mother complains and worries about her daughter's preference for men's work over women's. Her grandmother instructs her on the rules of appropriate and inappropriate behavior for young women. They long for the day when the narrator's brother, Laird, is old enough to take over the narrator's farm chores, forcing her indoors, where she belongs.

And gradually, the change does begin to occur. The narrator finds that her daydreams are changing. She no longer dreams of rescuing people from danger but dreams she is being rescued by a boy. She craves privacy from her brother; she wants to fix up her dressing table and make herself a skirt. In part, the narrator is being socialized, against her will, under the pressure of her mother and grandmother, into assuming the traditional female role. In part, she is embracing the changes and welcoming her transition into womanhood. One of the strengths of "Boys and Girls" is that its theme acknowledges the complexity of the assumption of gender roles. The narrator's transformation from tomboy to young woman is the product both of social forces and of her innate desire to become more feminine.

At the end of the story, the narrator liberates Flora, an old mare who is to be shot for fox meat. It is a symbolic act, though the narrator herself does not explain or fully understand the symbolism of her actions. It is, in part, an act of rebellion, a harbinger of the teenage years that are approaching. But it is more an act of defiance—she sets Flora free just as society is placing limits on her own freedom. Ironically, she is not punished for the action because, her father says, "She's only a girl." The strength of the effect of the first-person point of view is clear in the narrator's internal response to her father's comment: "I didn't protest that, even in my heart. Maybe it was true."

Robert Hayden, Those Winter Sundays

Narrative poems often employ the first-person point of view in dramatic monologues (see Chapter 2) or in autobiographical accounts of an experience that influenced the poet's values and ideals. Hayden's "Those Winter Sundays" is an autobiographical account of the poet's relationship with his father. The first-person viewpoint gives the poem its considerable emotional power.

The title alludes to cold Sunday mornings before church, when the poet's father woke up early, built a fire, and polished his son's good shoes. "No one ever thanked him" (line 5), the poet states. Indeed, the atmosphere in the house was hostile; the poet fears "the chronic angers of that house" (line 9). The poet and his father clearly did not get along. But he writes the poem from the perspective of an adult reflecting back on his childhood. As an adult, he realizes that his father's actions—warming up the house before the rest of the family arose, polishing the shoes—were acts of love, which went unacknowledged and unappreciated, and the poet now regrets his childhood indifference. "What did I know," he asks, as the poem ends, "what did I know / Of love's austere and lonely offices" (lines 13–14). These last lines, repeating the first-person pronoun "I," convey the full force of the first-person point of view, as the poet expresses his belated appreciation for his father's devotion to and love for his family.

THE FIRST-PERSON MINOR-CHARACTER NARRATOR

If the first-person major-character narrator is an egotist, the first-person minor-character narrator is a gossip. He or she observes the actions of another person, a friend, usually, and then tells the rest of us all about what that friend did, when, and to whom. Just as we like to tell stories that feature ourselves as the focus, we like to observe others and gossip about them. Stories told from the first-person minor-character point of view are interesting and engaging because the narrator openly puts his or her own spin on the personality and actions of the main character. Nick Carraway, the narrator of *The Great Gatsby,* discussed in the previous chapter, is a good example of a first-person minor-character narrator.

Doris Lessing, Our Friend Judith

Judith Castlewell is the main character of Doris Lessing's story "Our Friend Judith," but she is not the narrator. The narrator is an unnamed friend who gets the information that comprises the plot of the story from Judith herself and from another friend, Betty.

Judith is a single woman of 40, a poet, beautiful, independent, not particularly social. Her life is of great interest to Betty and the narrator because it is so different from their own and because Judith is such an interesting person. She lives her life the way she wants to, unencumbered by the usual responsibilities of a nine-to-five job and a demanding family. She travels to Italy on assignment for the BBC and meets Luigi, an Italian barber with whom she has a relationship. He becomes attached to her as does a pregnant cat, too young to have the three kittens she eventually gives birth to. The cat is unable to provide milk for her kittens and they die, one of them killed by the cat herself, one by Luigi. Judith is devastated by the whole experience. Unable or not knowing how to deal with so much emotional turmoil, she returns home to England, to the great disappointment of Luigi and his sister.

Although Judith is clearly the central character of the story, she could not be its narrator. In spite of her education and intelligence, Judith lacks self-knowledge. She is remote and detached from others, but, as the ending of the story makes clear, she sees herself as a more caring person than she really is. She appears quite indifferent to the sorrow she brings to Luigi and his family. Indeed, it is because she is an intellectual, more comfortable with affairs of the head than the heart, that she cannot fathom the interest others take in her. She could not be bothered to tell a story of which she is the center. Her friends are fascinated by Judith's personality and actions, always trying but never quite succeeding in understanding them. For this reason, the first-person minor-character works well for Lessing's story.

THE OBJECTIVE NARRATOR

Sometimes a writer will try to make his or her narrator disappear entirely and rely almost exclusively on dialogue among characters to tell the story. Much like a dramatist, the objective narrator establishes setting in a precise but rather detached style, and then lets the conversation tell the story.

Ernest Hemingway, Hills Like White Elephants

"Hills Like White Elephants" is a good example of the use of the objective point of view. The story is set in a train station in Spain, which Hemingway describes in a single terse paragraph. Thereafter, a conversation ensues between a young man and a young woman. Occasionally, the dialogue is interrupted by description that, suitably, reads more like stage directions than the voice of a narrator. The objective point of view does seem to turn a story into a play. Dialogue carries the story in which the young man tries to talk the woman into having an abortion so that they might maintain the same carefree lifestyle they have been enjoying for some time. The conversation is intense—the woman resists her lover's persuasive appeal, then she seems to relent, but her final decision remains deliberately ambiguous.

For stories like "Hills Like White Elephants," in which two characters vie to establish their positions within an intimate relationship, the objective point of view is very effective.

MULTIPLE POINTS OF VIEW

Novelists will sometimes use multiple points of view in their work. The effect can be disconcerting at first, but when done skillfully, it can add a whole new dimension to a story. It is disconcerting when an omniscient narrator suddenly takes a story over from a first-person narrator, because the abrupt shift can seem to interrupt the flow of the plot. Usually, though, any confusion is temporary, and the reader can soon connect a story told from one perspective to its continuation, told from another. A multiple viewpoint is also fascinating, in that the reader is given more than one perspective from which to view the events that comprise the story.

Charles Dickens, Bleak House

Bleak House tells an intricate, sweeping, and complex story—part satire, part murder mystery—rendered more accessible by its double point of view. Half of the novel is omniscient; half is first-person. The first-person narrator is Esther Summerson, housekeeper to John Jarndyce, who is guardian to Richard Carstone and Ada Clare. Richard and Ada are distant cousins, involved in a celebrated legal battle, which is one aspect of the book's plot and, as representative of the chaos of the legal system, a target of the book's satire. Ultimately, the case is settled, but all of the estate's assets have gone to legal costs, and Richard, who has secretly married Ada, dies in despair.

Dickens's attack on the legal system is also evident in the character of Tulkinghorn, lawyer to the aristocratic Dedlock family. One of the book's central mysteries is the relationship between Lady Dedlock and Captain Hawdon, also known as Nemo, who was once an army officer but who has fallen on hard times and has to eke out a living copying legal documents. Tulkinghorn tracks down Nemo because he had given Lady Dedlock a legal document Nemo had copied, and she had fainted when she recognized the handwriting. Tulkinghorn finds Nemo, dead of an opium overdose, but learns about his past with the help of Detective Bucket. They discover that Lady Dedlock and Captain Hawdon were lovers and that Esther is their daughter. Esther was raised by her aunt, Miss Barbary, who has told her sister that Esther died in childbirth. John Jarndyce eventually employs Esther as his housekeeper and as a companion to his ward and cousin, Ada.

Jarndyce's best friend, Lawrence Boythorn, lives next door to the Dedlocks, and Esther meets her mother (though she is unaware of their relationship at this time) when the Jarndyce household spends some time visiting Mr. Boythorn. By now Tulkinghorn has tracked down letters proving that Esther is the illegitimate daughter of Lady Dedlock and Nemo. Lady Dedlock learns the truth and tells Esther but on condition that the secret is never revealed. However, she learns that Tulkinghorn is planning to reveal the secret, and she plans to leave her home in Chesney Wold to spare her prominent husband the humiliation that her past would cause him. Tulk-inghorn is murdered by Lady Dedlock's maid Hortense but by now Lady Dedlock has fled and does not know her secret died with her meddlesome lawyer. Detective Bucket, who solved the mystery of Tulkinghorn's death, finds her dead at the gate of the churchyard where Nemo lies buried.

Esther, meanwhile, has fallen in love with a young doctor and he has fallen in love with her. They marry and move to Yorkshire. Ada and her child continue to live under the care of John Jarndyce.

The double point of view of *Bleak House* intensifies the theme of the novel and increases the range of its satire. Dickens's theme is that England is falling apart, the victim of a corrupt legal system, whose primary function is to make work for itself; the victim of religious hypocrisy; and the victim of misplaced idealism. The omniscient narrator, detached and unemotional, reports in the present tense on the sorry state of the nation without critical comment: This is the way things are. But Esther, as first-person past-tense narrator, offers a chance of counteracting social despair through her simple gentility and acts of Christian charity: This is the way things can be if we treat each other with dignity and respect. Through his double narrative, then, Dickens can present a detached view of the problem and a personal view of the solution.

By contrasting Esther's compassion with the hypocrisy rampant within her society, Dickens also intensifies the force of his satire. The character of Mrs. Jellyby represents mis-placed idealism, as she raises money for the poor in Africa while completely neglecting the welfare of her own family who Esther has to rescue. The young street sweeper, Jo, is similarly ignored, indeed shunned, by those self-proclaimed Christians who should come to his aid. Again, it is only Es-ther and Dr. Woodcourt who show him any real kindness.

England, Dickens seems to be saying, is a bleak house, with one room filled with faith, hope, and charity; and many rooms filled with hopelessness and despair, products of a tangled legal system and a church that has abandoned its Christian mission. From above, the omniscient narrator tells the story of the bleak house that is England. From that sin-gle room in the house, Esther tells the story that reflects Dick-ens's own hope for a liberal humanist value system, which will reform the great social institutions, especially the law.

Setting

Compared to character (Chapter 5) and point of view (Chapter 6), setting is a straightforward literary element that simply establishes the **time when** and the **place where** the action of a story, play, or poem occurs. Yet setting can have as important an influence on the meaning of a literary work as any other literary element. Setting can be as important to plot (Chapter 4) as character. It can serve a symbolic (Chapter 11) function and resonate with connotations beyond its time and place. Setting can also contribute to the irony (Chapter 4) of a story. The influence of setting on plot, symbolism, irony, and metaphor is explored in this chapter.

SETTING AND PLOT

The community in which we live can influence our personalities and our actions. People who are from small towns think people from big cities are harried and rather rude; people from major cities think small-towners are slow and rather simple. Similarly, citizens of one country tend to have different values and attitudes than citizens of another, and when we travel to another place, our behavior is usually mediated by local history, culture, and custom. In other words, the time and place (the setting) where the action (the plot) occurs influences human events and behavior.

Sinclair Ross, The Painted Door

During winter, snow rising to farmhouse rooftops defines, in part, the setting of the Canadian Prairie. "The Painted Door" is set amid a Prairie blizzard, and it is this unrelenting and ominous snowfall that determines the direction the plot of the story takes.

John, a Prairie farmer, must walk five miles to his father's farm to check on him because the weather has been so bad. John's wife, Ann, is bitter, not wanting to be alone. John promises to stop by their friend Stephen's house and ask him to visit and keep Ann company. John will be home by early evening and they can play cards together. To pass the time before Stephen arrives, Ann begins to paint the bedroom. Stephen arrives and they wait for John. But this blizzard is ferocious and, as time passes, they decide John will have stayed the night with his father and not have risked the danger of so long a walk in such desperate weather. Ann yields to her despair over her lot in life, her best years sacrificed to the constant toil of the farmer's wife, and she lets Stephen spend the night with her. She awakens at midnight, overcome with a nightmare that John had returned home and caught them. In the morning, she awakens, chastened, and resolves to atone for her sin by becoming a model farmer's wife. But John's body is discovered, frozen, his hands still clasping his own wire fence. Apparently he had set off to return home but did not quite make it. His body is brought into the house, and, as Ann examines her husband, she notices on his hand a smear of the paint she was using to paint their bedroom.

The setting of this story, dominated by the landscape of snow the fierce blizzard produces, determines the direction the plot takes. Metaphorically, the snow hides Stephen and Ann's infidelity. It also presents a challenge to John to prove his devotion to his wife by making it home, as he promised he would. He does make it home. He conquers the elements to prove his love for his wife. But he returns to the snow and succumbs to the blizzard when he discovers the devotion is one-sided.

William Trevor, Beyond the Pale

"Beyond the Pale" is set in Ireland but its main characters are English. When an author places English people in an Irish setting, the setting will likely influence the plot because of the historical relationship between those two countries.

The story is about four bridge partners who holiday together each year at an idyllic Irish country inn. To these four comfortably-off English people, Ireland is a utopia, and "the troubles" (the historical animosities between Catholics and Protestants) do not exist. The relationships among the bridge partners is complex. Strafe is married to Cynthia but has an open affair with Dorothy, the first-person minor-character (see Chapter 6) narrator of the story. Strafe leaves the room he shares with his wife and visits Dorothy in her room on a regular basis. Cynthia is supposed to turn a blind eye to her husband's infidelity, as all of them turn a blind eye to the Irish-Catholic struggle for independence and the social consequences of that struggle. But, on this visit, politics enters paradise when another hotel guest befriends Cynthia and tells her about his childhood sweetheart who moved to London to plant bombs for the IRA. A bomb she was building exploded and killed her. Later, overwrought by the tragedy, the guest wanders into the ocean and drowns himself.

At first, Cynthia is devastated by the experience, but, as she recovers, she confronts the truth. Her first truth is the responsibility she and her countrymen share for the civil war in Ireland and for the agony it has caused. Cynthia becomes conscious of her setting not as an idyllic holiday resort but as a real place with social problems she and her bridge partners, representatives of the English middle class, have ignored for too long. Her second truth is that, by ignoring her husband's infidelity with a supposed friend, she has lost her own self-respect. She recovers it in the course of an intensely dramatic confrontation scene at the end of the story.

In "Beyond the Pale," the setting incites the development of the political dimension of the plot, which, in turn, results in Cynthia's personal liberation. The narrator, Dorothy, refuses to acknowledge either Irish politics or the significance of Cynthia's outburst, which she regards as the ravings of a mad woman.

The British, Trevor seems to be saying, are making progress, but there are many still who believe the problem will go away if they ignore it. Cynthia proves the English can overcome their indifference to their relationship with Ireland; but Dorothy believes the solution is to blame the victim.

Robert Browning, Porphyria's Lover

The plot of "Porphyria's Lover" is also influenced by the setting. The setting is established in the first four lines:

The rain set early in to-night
The sullen wind was soon awake,
It tore the elm-tops down for spite,
And did its worst to vex the lake:

It is the stereotypical dark and stormy night, a night when reason loses its edge and irrational passion prevails. It is a night when a psychotic killer can murder his lover so that he can possess her forever.

Escaping from the severe storm, Porphyria enters her lover's cottage. Her lover, who narrates the poem, is thrilled with Porphyria's devotion to him:

> . . . at last I knew
> Porphyria worshipp'd me; surprise
> Made my heart swell, and still it grew
> While I debated what to do.
> That moment she was mine, mine, fair,
> Perfectly pure and good...
> (lines 32–37)

What he does at this moment when he is certain of Porphyria's devotion is to strangle her, apparently to freeze and make permanent the moment he had longed for. On such a night, such wickedness seems acceptable. It is as if God has gone to sleep. The poem ends:

> And all night long we have not stirr'd,
> And yet God has not said a word.
> (lines 59–60)

SETTING AND SYMBOLISM

In some works of literature, the setting is more than the time and the place. It suggests a condition or a desire that transcends the where and the when of the action; in other words, the setting can serve a symbolic function.

Robert Frost, Stopping by Woods on a Snowy Evening

The setting of Frost's much-anthologized poem "Stopping by Woods on a Snowy Evening" is clearly established by the poem's title. The narrator of the poem stops to appreciate the beauty of a winter night in the New England woods, comments on how he would like to remain, then, realizing he has "promises to keep / And miles to go before I sleep" (lines 15–16), continues on his journey.

Some literary critics feel the dark woods specifically symbolize death, and that the poem's narrator is, in fact, contemplating suicide. He feels guilty about stopping, his horse is agitated, it is "the darkest evening of the year" (line 8), and the woods are "dark and deep" (line 13). Moreover, the repetition of the last line implies a "sleep" beyond a single night. In the end, the narrator rejects death, symbolized by the macabre appeal the dark woods have for him, knowing that too many people depend upon him.

Ernest Hemingway, The Snows of Kilimanjaro

"The Snows of Kilimanjaro" is set on the hot African plain where the protagonist, Harry, has gone with his wife for a hunting expedition. But what started as a scratch in his leg turns gangrenous, and medical help is many miles away. As Harry lies waiting for help, he reflects upon his life with his wife. Her wealth, he rather selfishly believes, has inhibited his talent as a writer, destroyed his motivation to write, and now, likely dying, he cannot hide his bitterness toward her. Throughout the story, he reflects upon significant experiences in his life he always wanted to write about but now will not. His flashbacks become delusional as the gangrene spreads. Finally, he imagines he is being rescued. A pilot has come to take him to safety. But instead of flying him to safety, the pilot takes him toward the snowcapped peaks of Mount Kilimanjaro. Back at the camp on the plain, a hyena, which has stalked Harry throughout the story, makes a strange crying sound. Harry's wife wakes up and discovers her husband dead in his cot.

The setting of this story, the hot African plain where Harry lies dying of gangrene, symbolizes Harry's own arid life, at least as he sees it. His imagination is alive with ideas for stories but he has quit writing, content to live a pampered life, courtesy of his wife's fortune. The gangrene suggests the corruption of his talent.

The other primary though imaginary setting of the story, the snowcapped peaks of Kilimanjaro, are also symbolic. They contrast the hot African plain; they are clean and pure; they represent the goal toward which Harry should have striven. Instead of dying struggling to reach the summit, Harry has let wealth render him bitter and indolent. He has squandered his talent and has died of gangrene on the arid plains of Africa. Had he used and cultivated his talent, he might, metaphorically, have soared to the heights of Kilimanjaro.

William Blake, London

The London of Blake's poem represents all of the chaos and distress that even now we associate with life in a busy and hectic metropolis.

The poem's narrator wanders through the busy London streets and sees the stress and despair etched into the faces of the people who pass him by:

> And mark in every face I meet
> Marks of weakness, marks of woe.
> (lines 3–4)

The people seem oppressed by the laws that metaphorically imprison them (the "mind-forged manacles" of line 8),
instead of setting them free. The city is corrupted by the exploitation of child labor, by the mighty institutions of government, which have on their hands the blood shed by
soldiers whom the politicians have sent to fight and die for
their country. But what appalls Blake's narrator the most are
the young streetwalkers whose poverty has forced them
into a life that produces unwanted children—"Blasts the
newborn Infant's tear" (line 15)—and that spreads sexually-
transmitted disease that destroys marriage: "And blights
with plagues the Marriage hearse" (line 16).

Blake's poem symbolizes the universality of certain settings. Set in eighteenth-century London, Blake's poem, with
a few changes in its diction, could describe not only the
eighteenth-century London Blake clearly knew so well, but
a contemporary Western city as well.

SETTING AND IRONY

The setting adds to the irony of a literary work when there
is a disconnect between that setting and the events taking
place within it. It is ironic when a murder occurs in a church
or when a war breaks out on Christmas day.

Henry Reed, Naming of Parts

"Naming of Parts" is set in springtime amidst Japonica
glistening "like coral" (line 5), silent almond blossoms, and
fragrant flowers. It is a perfect setting for romance or peaceful contemplation. Instead, the Royal Army Ordinance Corps
(in which Reed served) is in training to fight in World War II
and is learning the names of the parts of their rifles under
the command of a stern and humorless sergeant major.

In this juxtaposition between an Edenic setting and a lesson on the naming of the parts of a rifle, Reed conveys the antiwar theme, typical of much of his poetry.

Shirley Jackson, The Lottery

"The Lottery" is set on the morning of June 27, in a small
idyllic town in middle America. Everybody knows everybody
else, and they interact in that friendly good-humored manner
that characterizes the American small town. On this day,
June 27, they are preparing for an annual celebration, a lottery, the purpose of which is not immediately clear. There
seems to be something ominous about it, however, since the
children are gathering together piles of stones. One of the

townspeople mentions some talk about giving up the lottery, but he is silenced by another who reminds the dissenter of the old saying, "Lottery in June, corn be heavy soon."

As the saying suggests, the lottery is based on the ancient belief that the community must make a sacrifice to the fertility gods in order to assure a good crop. Once a year, this community conducts a savage fertility ritual, that involves a human sacrifice. Each citizen in the town is given a piece of paper, on one of which is a black dot. The hapless person who has "won" the lottery is then stoned to death by his or her friends and neighbors, who believe their livelihood depends upon appeasing the gods responsible for their crop.

In her story, Jackson harshly satirizes communities that cling to traditions simply because they are traditional, even when they deny logic and reason to say nothing of charity and compassion. The irony that suffuses this story is the result of the juxtaposition between the idyllic setting and the savage ritual that occurs within its boundaries.

T. S. Eliot, The Waste Land

Eliot's famous poem *The Waste Land* contains many settings, virtually all of which are symbolic in allusive and complex ways. The poem is a montage of apparently disjointed scenes and descriptions, set in Munich, London, Egypt, Smyrna, and India. An amazing array of people wander through the poem: fortune-tellers, businesspeople, working-class men and women drinking in pubs, Cleopatra, Tiresias, Queen Elizabeth I, Phoenician sailors. The poem is written in free verse, which contains excerpts of working-class dialogue, babble, and passages of great lyrical beauty. The many dimensions of the poem are united by its common theme: the spiritual decay of modern life and the need for faith to revitalize the collective will of humankind, crushed by the horrors of World War I.

The poem is divided into five parts. Part 1, "The Burial of the Dead," opens with the famous lines:

April is the cruelest month, breeding
Lilacs out of the dead land . . .
(lines 1–2)

The lines parody the opening of Geoffrey Chaucer's *The Canterbury Tales,* which begins by celebrating April as the sweetest not the cruelest month because it heralds the arrival of spring, the renewal of life, the start of a religious pilgrimage. Eliot's point is that postwar Europe has become a wasteland where no such regeneration is possible. Images and symbols of drought, death, and despair recur in this part in several settings, suggesting the spiritual malaise that has gripped the world. *The Waste Land* has many settings, but it is set primarily in London, which Eliot describes at the end of Part 1, in a manner suggesting Blake's London discussed above:

> Unreal City,
> Under the brown fog of a winter dawn, so many,
> I had not thought death had undone so many.
> (lines 60–62)

Part 2, "A Game of Chess," begins with an ironic paraphrase of Shakespeare's description of Cleopatra on her throne. It shifts to "rats' alley / Where the dead men lost their bones" (lines 115–116). It ends in a pub amidst gossip about soldiers coming back from the war, false teeth, and abortion. Like all of the poem, this part conveys the impression of human vanity, stress, death, and sorrow, unrelieved by faith or hope.

Part 3 is called "The Fire Sermon," in reference to the Buddha's warning about the dangers of substituting lust for love. It describes a London, desolate and deserted by all except that rat, which makes an encore appearance, "Dragging its slimy belly on the bank" (line 188). The soothsayer Tiresias appears and, echoing the Fire Sermon, describes a couple whose brief sexual encounter is devoid of any feeling. Meanwhile, on the Thames, Queen Elizabeth I flirts with the Earl of Leicester, but their relationship, like all in *The Waste Land,* is political and manipulative, not joyous and restorative.

The brief fourth part of the poem is entitled "Death by Water." Water is a traditional symbol of life, suggesting as it does the spiritual initiation of baptism. But this is the waste land and here water is scarce and what there is drowns one of the poem's characters, Phlebas the Phoenician sailor.

The water image is continued in the fifth and final part of the poem, "What the Thunder Said." Significantly, this wasteland thunder brings noise but little rain. This part of the poem is set on the road to Emmaus and suggests Christ's journey to Gethsemane. The focus is on Christ's imprisonment and trial, his crucifixion and the hopeless days before his resurrection. Images of barren landscapes, war, satanic women, and empty chapels reverberate throughout this section. Then the thunder speaks, bringing a message of hope. Alluding to a Hindu fable, Eliot has the thunder announce the need for charity, sympathy, and compassion. The message falls upon deaf ears. There is a sense more of self-ishness than charity, amidst a world that is crumbling.

> I sat upon the shore
> Fishing, with the arid plain behind me
> Shall I at least set my lands in order?
> London Bridge is falling down falling down falling
> down.
> (lines 424–427).

The poem ends optimistically, to an extent, with the suggestion that religious virtues can restore the wasted land, but the will to embrace these virtues seems absent.

Clearly, *The Waste Land* is a very ironic, symbolic, allusive, and in some ways elusive poem. Its many diverse settings have symbolic and ironic overtones. Much of the poem is set in the desert, which mirrors the spiritual drought that has gripped postwar Europe. Much of the poem is set in a London whose citizens symbolize the confusion and despair that come when faith has been abandoned. The last part of the poem seems to be set, at least in part, in places wherein the poem's irony and symbolism climax: the Garden of Gethsemane, the scene of Christ's agony, and Gogotha where Christ was crucified.

SETTING AND METAPHOR

A metaphor (discussed in detail in Chapter 9) is a comparison, the purpose of which is to clarify or intensify the more complex of the objects being compared. When we read Plutarch's words "poetry is painting that speaks," we understand more clearly what Plutarch means and how he feels about poetry.

William Shakespeare, Full Many a Glorious Morning Have I Seen

In his 33rd sonnet, "Full Many a Glorious Morning Have I Seen," Shakespeare compares the literal sun to the sunshine of his own life, his great friend, who inspired his sonnet sequence. The sun in the sky shines brightly, the poet says, but can be eclipsed by a single cloud. Similarly, the poet's friend can shine the light of his friendship on the poet, but then turn his attention to someone else. We would expect the poet to be crushed by his friend's fickleness, but the poet takes his metaphor to its more logical conclusion. If the sun in the heavens can be blotted out, he says, I can hardly expect my earthly sun to shine only for me:

Yet him for this my love no whit disdaineth;
Suns of the world may stain when heaven's sun
staineth.
(lines 13–14)

The sonnet's setting, then, is used as a metaphor for a
friend's devotion.

Thomas Hardy, The Darkling Thrush

Hardy's poem is set on the day it was composed, Decem-
ber 31, 1900. It is the dusk of a most dreary and desolate
evening. To the speaker, the inclement day is a metaphor for
the whole sad century now coming to an end:

The land's sharp features seemed to be
The Century's corpse outleant,
His crypt the cloudy canopy,
The wind his death-lament.
(lines 9–12)

It is a metaphor, as well, for his own fervorless mood:

The ancient pulse of germ and birth
Was shrunken hard and dry,
And every spirit upon earth
Seemed fervorless as I.
(lines 13–16)

Suddenly, the poet hears the joyful song of an old thrush.
He cannot fathom the cause for joy amidst "the growing
gloom" (line 24). The song cannot alleviate his own despair,
which the landscape continues to reflect, but he does acknowledge the possibility of "Some blessed Hope" (line 31).
Hardy's is a common poetic metaphor. Winter is a
metaphor for the decay of the human spirit, but just as spring
supersedes winter, hope can triumph over despair.

Yvor Winters, At the San Francisco Airport

Winters' poem is set at a terminal in the San Francisco
Airport. The poem is dedicated to the poet's daughter who
is leaving home, probably going to a university. The poet is
saying goodbye to her and reflecting upon the meaning of
the experience. He is protective of his daughter still, even
while he recognizes that he is "the past, and that is all" (line
10). He is conflicted, knowing children must leave home, yet
recognizing how her departure redefines his own role as an
adult, his own passage through life. He is sad but resigned
to the inevitability of a reality all parents must face. He is
lonely:

This is the terminal, the break.
Beyond this point, on lines of air,
You take the way that you must take;
And I remain in light and stare—
In light, and nothing else, awake.
(lines 21–25)

The poem's dominant metaphor is its setting. The airport suggests departure and change, suggestions that are heightened by Winters' emphasis on the double entendre of the word "terminal," which he introduces in the first stanza of his five-stanza poem and repeats in the last. To the poet, the airport terminal suggests the beginning of the end, but, to his daughter, it represents the end of the beginning.

William Shakespeare, A Midsummer Night's Dream

Shakespeare's often-staged comedy, *A Midsummer Night's Dream,* has two main settings. The metaphorical energy of these settings and the ways in which these settings are juxtaposed create much of the dynamism of the play's plot and help to define the characters.

The play opens in Athens amidst preparations for a royal marriage of Queen Hippolyta to Duke Theseus. A prominent Athenian citizen, Egeus, interrupts the plans to appeal to the duke to settle a dispute he is having with his daughter, Hermia. Hermia wants to marry Lysander but her father insists she marry Demetrius. The duke sides with Egeus: Hermia must marry Demetrius.

Lysander and Hermia decide to elope and agree to meet in the woods on the outskirts of Athens. Here is the play's other main setting: the enchanted forest. It exists beyond the city where humans make and enforce harsh laws designed to assure proper behavior among young people. It is a supernatural world of sprites and fairies, of magic and anarchy.

It is not, however, without conflict. Oberon, the King of the Fairies, is feuding with his Queen, Titania, who has adopted a beautiful young boy whom Oberon wants as a page. Titania refuses to give up the boy. Oberon commissions the mischievous sprite Puck to bewitch Titania so that she will give him his page boy.

Meanwhile, Demetrius enters the enchanted forest searching for Hermia and Lysander. He has learned of their plot courtesy of Helena, Hermia's friend and confidant. Helena revealed her friend's secret to curry favor with Demetrius who she loves, despite the fact that he loves Hermia.

Helena follows Demetrius and professes her love but Demetrius spurns her. Oberon observes the exchange and feels sorry for Helena.

Oberon orders Puck to find a potion, which Oberon will dab onto Titania's eyes. The potion will distract Titania, by forcing her to fall hopelessly in love with the next creature she looks upon, at which time Oberon will steal the young boy from her. He also orders Puck to anoint Demetrius's eyes with the same potion at such a time that he will awaken and see Helena and thereby return her love.

The elopers, Lysander and Hermia, now arrive in the enchanted forest. They are lost and tired and lie down to rest. Puck mistakes Lysander for Demetrius and sprinkles the magic potion onto Lysander's eyes. Helena arrives and awakens Lysander who, of course, promptly falls hopelessly in love with her. Helena believes he is mocking her and she flees.

Now a group of Athenian craftsmen are also in the forest to rehearse a play that they plan to perform in honor of the duke's marriage. The mischievous Puck turns one of the craftsmen, Bottom the Weaver, into an ass, and Bottom's friends run away terrified. Titania, sleeping nearby, awakens to see the ass and, under the influence of the magic potion, promptly falls hopelessly in love with him. Bottom can barely believe his luck.

Oberon is overjoyed at his success with bewitching Titania but scolds Puck for his error and takes matters into his own hands by anointing Demetrius's eyes with the magic potion himself. But when Demetrius awakens he, too, sees Helena and falls in love with her. Helena, pursued now by both men, still thinks she is the victim of a practical joke and that her erstwhile best friend, Hermia, is in on it. The women are about to come to blows, as are the men. Puck loves the confusion he has caused, but Oberon scolds him and orders him to undo his mischief.

Meanwhile Titania gladly hands over her young boy to Oberon and continues to dote on Bottom the Weaver, always figuratively but for now, literally, an ass. Having won, Oberon breaks the spell on Titania with whom he now reconciles. Puck has also straightened things out at last so that Lysander is back in love with Hermia and Demetrius is now in love with Helena. Puck has also given Bottom back his humanity, and he reunites with his friends to continue their rehearsal.

The duke sanctions the marriage of Lysander to Hermia, Demetrius to Helena, and joyfully anticipates a triple wedding, his own to Hippolyta being the third.

The wedding entertainment, the performance of *Pyramus and Thisbe* by the Athenian craftsmen, is, predictably, a fiasco, but most of the members of the audience are tolerant and more concerned, anyway, with celebrating the marriages than in criticizing a dramatic performance. As the play ends, the mortals leave and the supernatural creatures appear and promise to visit each bridal chamber to bless the union of the three couples.

At the end of the play, then, the dreamworld of the enchanted forest inhabited by supernatural beings enters the real world of ordinary mortals just as, earlier in the play, the mortals invaded the enchanted forest. This interrelationship, between the natural and the supernatural, is, of course, part of Shakespeare's point. *A Midsummer Night's Dream* is a love story. Love is a natural experience, which often assumes supernatural dimensions. Young people fall in and out of love whimsically. Demetrius and Lysander are inconstant lovers both in love with Hermia one minute and Helena the next, until they finally sort out who best belongs with whom. The transformations are magical; it's as if they are bewitched, so capriciously do they behave.

Shakespeare reinforces this capriciousness through his metaphorical use of settings. The enchanted forest represents both the inconstancy and the magic of romance, a mood reinforced by a magic potion, which can make even a queen fall in love with a donkey. Athens represents order, parental authority, the authority of the state, none of which is conducive to romantic love. But the borders of these settings are not secure. Sprites visit Athens and Athenians play in the enchanted forest. Shakespeare places no value judgments upon his settings; he privileges neither the order of the city nor the merriment of Puck's woods. Through his metaphorical use of settings, Shakespeare reminds us that love represents both a serious commitment sanctioned by dukes and fathers and a joyful celebration, catered by the residents of a magic kingdom.

8

Theme

Answer these three questions: What things in life are most important to you? What are the most significant social issues of our time? What stages do most people pass through in the course of a lifetime? Your answers—family, faith, work, friends, intimate relationships, education; war, poverty, ecology; childhood, adolescence, marriage, parenthood, old age, death—identify the common topics of literature. Most poems, stories, and plays come with a message, often more than one, about an important issue. Authors usually try to enlighten their readers as well as entertain them. Writers relate the complete variety of human experience and try, in the process, to give their readers some insight into the significance of that experience. The literary term for the message, the insight into human experience an author offers to his or her readers, is **theme.** In this chapter, seven of the most common literary themes are described, and illustrated with reference to widely taught poems or stories.

FAMILY

Since family is our basic social unit, it stands to reason writers will often tell of the love and conflict, the function and the dysfunction, inevitably found within any family.

St. Luke, The Parable of the Prodigal Son

In this, one of the oldest and most famous stories about fathers and sons, a son, the younger of two, asks his father for his share of the family estate. The father accedes. The son promptly leaves home, journeys to another country, "and there wasted his substance with riotous living" (Luke 15:13). Now broke, the younger son is reduced to working on a farm, feeding swine. Unable to endure the work, he decides to return home and offer himself as a servant on his father's estate. His father is overjoyed to see him and will not hear of him working as a servant. Instead, he slaughters a fatted calf, and throws a party to welcome his young son home. The older son is miffed. "Lo these many years," he says to his father, "do I serve thee, neither transgressed I at any time thy commandment: and yet thou never gavest me a kid, that I might make merry with my friends" (Luke 15:29). The father then gives his older son a lesson in tolerance and forgiveness. You will have all that is left of the estate, he reminds his older son. We must forgive your brother and celebrate his return, "for this thy brother was dead, and is alive again: and was lost, and is found" (Luke 15:32).

The father's words form the theme of the story. Family members forgive other family members who transgress, help family members who have fallen on hard times, and open the door to family members who want to come home, regardless of the circumstances under which they left. Within a family, this story reminds us, love is given without conditions.

Theodore Roethke, My Papa's Waltz

"My Papa's Waltz" is one of those fascinating poems that can be read in two, almost diametrically opposite ways, the choice dependent, usually, upon the reader's own experiences and perspective. The family described in Roethke's poem is either warm and loving or violent and abusive depending upon how readers perceive the nature of the events that Roethke describes.

The incident the poem recounts involves a father who comes home drunk and roughhouses with his son while a concerned mother/wife looks on. The father is clearly a hard-working man with his hand "battered on one knuckle" (line 10) and his palm "caked hard by dirt" (line 14). How does the young boy respond to his father? Some of the language Roethke uses suggests the boy is thrilled to be playing with his dad who energetically waltzes him around the kitchen. The poet uses the verb "romped" (line 5), which connotes fun. But the boy hangs on "like death" (line 3), suggesting that he fears his father's violence. The father clearly has been drinking as the first line—"The whiskey on your breath"—indicates. But the boy is "waltzed off to bed" (line 15), a line that again connotes enjoyment. He is "clinging" to his father's shirt (line 15), perhaps in terror or perhaps because he does not want to let go and end the fun. The mother is frowning, but is it a tolerant boys-will-be-boys frown as her men knock her pans off the kitchen shelf (lines 5–6); or is it a frown of concern for the safety of her son?

There is, of course, a compromise position. Perhaps the father is capable of violence, which the boy fears while, at the same time, he enjoys the attention and the rough play he is having with his dad. "My Papa's Waltz" speaks to the complex nature of a family dynamic, wherein love and abuse can, and, indeed, often do, coexist.

Katherine Mansfield, The Daughters of the Late Colonel

In "The Daughters of the Late Colonel," Katherine Mansfield describes the relationship between a father and his two daughters. The girls fear their father, a retired army colonel, who has totally dominated their lives. His death will change their lives, although they are not certain exactly how. They have completely lost their ability to assert themselves. The father's nurse exploits their kindness, and their maid is insolent and indifferent to their needs. As the story ends, they hear a noisy organ grinder and their immediate response is to rush outside and give the organ grinder money so he will move on quickly and not disturb their father. They realize suddenly they don't have to live their lives catering to their father's every need and whim as they had in the past. Clearly the sudden freedom has confused them, and it might even be too late for them to adjust to the new life their father's death offers.

A theme of "The Daughters of the Late Colonel" is that parents wield considerable power in shaping their children's personalities, and that parents who are too authoritarian can mold children into adults unable to stand up for themselves.

Richard Wilbur, The Writer

The narrator of this poem pauses on his stairwell to listen to the sound of a typewriter, which his daughter is using to write a story. He is struck by the realization that she has things to write about, that even her young life "is a great cargo, and some of it heavy" (line 8). To himself, he wishes her "a lucky passage" (line 9). For a moment, there is silence, then the typing resumes, and there is silence again. The father recalls an incident that happened two years previously: A starling was trapped in his daughter's room, and they watched together in concern until the bird found the open window and escaped. The bird's struggle to escape becomes a metaphor for the daughter's struggle to write her story. The father appreciates even more now his daughter's effort. In its way, it is as intense as their bird's struggle to escape.

The theme of the poem is a father's love for his daughter. More specifically, the father realizes that his daughter's life will be a struggle sometimes, and that, as much as he wants to help her, he cannot; his daughter must take wing and fly all by herself.

Jamaica Kincaid, Girl

"Girl" is a brief short story, occupying not much more than a page of the many literature anthologies in which it appears. It is set in the West Indies where Kincaid grew up. It is, in a sense, a prose dramatic monologue (see Chapter 2). The story consists of a speech a West Indian mother gives to her daughter, rattling off advice on everything from domestic duties to acceptable public behavior. Her tone is blunt, even dictatorial. She will not tolerate back talk and ignores or challenges the two brief remarks her daughter does manage to squeeze in.

The mother does not come across as warm and loving. She comes across as a woman more concerned about what her neighbors will say than about her daughter's own feelings. She seems especially worried about her daughter's apparent sexual proclivities:

> . . . on Sundays try to walk like a lady and not like the slut you are so bent on becoming.
>
>   . . .
>
> . . . this is how to behave in the presence of men who don't know you very well, and this way they won't recognize immediately the slut I've warned you against becoming.

These are harsh, even cruel words, which create that spiteful tone consistent throughout the story.

One theme of "Girl" is the pressure to conform that society places on a family, and the stress this social pressure can create. Children resent parents who seem more concerned about what others will think of them than about their own emotional well-being.

Amy Tan, Two Kinds

"Two Kinds" is another mother-daughter relationship story, this time one colored by the influence of culture. The mother is a Chinese woman somewhat influenced by American culture; the daughter, Jing-Mei, is the child of Chinese parents but is an American, somewhat influenced by Chinese culture. The cultural gap between the two of them provides the primary source of conflict in the story.

Mother is convinced daughter can be a child prodigy—this is America, after all. She tries to transform her daughter into the Chinese Shirley Temple. She gives Jing-Mei memory tests. She forces her to take piano lessons. Each attempt is more painful and humiliating than the one before, though Tan undercuts Jing-Mei's agony by effectively exploring the humor in the situations she describes. After a recital that is a disaster, Jing-Mei puts her foot down and angrily refuses to play the piano any longer. She sees her conflict with her mother in cultural terms:

> And then I decided. I didn't have to do what my mother said anymore. I wasn't her slave. This wasn't China.

Her relationship with her mother is transformed forever when Jing-Mei, furious, reminds her of her twin daughters abandoned in China after the revolution and now likely dead. They don't truly reconcile until the mother offers Jing-Mei the piano as a thirtieth-birthday present.

The theme of "Two Kinds" is intensified by the story's cultural conflict, by the Asian determination to succeed clashing with American nonchalance. But, insofar as the story is about parents determined to have their children realize the potential parents are convinced their children have, its theme is universal.

Sharon Olds, The Planned Child

This poem explores the theme of family love more from the child's rather than from the parents' perspective. The narrator begins by expressing regret that her parents had planned her so calculatingly. Her mother charted her temperature so that she would know the optimal time to conceive. The narrator is disappointed. She would have liked a more romantic story. She "would have / liked to have been conceived in heat / in haste, by mistake, in love, in sex . . ." (lines 6–8). But then a friend recognizes in the narrator a special quality that suggests the narrator was "a child who had been wanted" (line 11). Immediately, the narrator's perspective changes. The world was not enough for her parents without her in it. For all of its natural glory, "Orion / cartwheeling across the dark" (lines 19–20), the world was not enough for them unless they had her with them. She is pleased now to be the Planned Child.

A theme of this poem is that a love child suggests the passion between the child's parents while a planned child proves a mother's love for her baby.

LOVE

Love is another common literary theme. Most writers, poets especially, have paid tribute in verse to the man or woman they love.

Elizabeth Barrett Browning, How Do I Love Thee

One of the most famous of such tributes is Elizabeth Barrett Browning's sonnet, "How Do I Love Thee," written to express her love for her husband, Robert. Her poem expresses a common sentiment in poems of this nature: Our love is not merely physical; it is righteous and spiritual, as well:

I love thee freely, as men strive for Right;
I love thee purely, as they turn from praise.
(lines 7–8)

Barrett Browning's theme is that true love is a spiritual union of two souls, a union that will last forever.

Leonard Cohen, Dance Me to the End of Love

Cohen's poem reads like a marriage proposal, like the words of a man who wants to spend the rest of his life with the woman to whom the poem is addressed. In the course of the poem, the narrator expresses his sexual attraction to his intended, his gratitude for the woman's ability to soothe the stress ("the panic," line 3) that is in his life, and his desire to raise a family with her. The poem's title, repeated at the end of each stanza, suggests his conviction that their relationship will last until the end of their lives.

E. E. Cummings, somewhere i have never travelled

Cummings' poem is addressed to a loved one who is possibly a partner or even possibly a child. Certainly, the person addressed is small and frail, though cummings does not use "frail" in any pejorative sense. Indeed, it is, paradoxically, a source of the power this person has over the narrator:

nothing which we are to perceive in this world equals
the power of your intense fragility: whose texture
compels me with the color of its countries,
rendering death and forever with each breathing
(lines 13–16)

This is someone who affects the narrator as no one else does. He can open up to this person though he is, by nature, someone who seems to find intimacy difficult.

Typically of a cummings poem, this one is full of striking metaphors that are puzzling on a literal level but comprehensible metaphorically. In the second-to-last line of this twenty-line poem, for example, cummings mixes metaphors as only a poet could: "the voice of your eyes is deeper than all roses." Another startling but effective comparison appears in the last line: "nobody, not even the rain, has such small hands."

Cummings' diction, his serene tone, and his unusual metaphors combine to convey the sense of a man captivated by power that the person he is addressing has over him.

William Butler Yeats, The Folly of Being Comforted

The poems discussed so far in this section are all expressions of love from one person to another. "The Folly of Being Comforted" is, by contrast, a poem of unrequited love. It opens with words from the narrator's friend who thinks he is bringing good news about the woman with whom the narrator seems obsessed. This woman, the friend says, is losing her beauty. She is growing old; her hair is graying; lines are noticeable around her eyes. Be patient, the friend says, and your love will fade. The narrator responds, telling his friend he does not know what he is talking about. Age is enhancing, not diminishing her beauty because she grows even more noble as time passes. If she would but turn her head and notice me, I would be a happy man and you would understand your folly in trying to comfort me.

"The Folly of Being Comforted" is a rather sad poem about a man hopelessly in love with a woman who does not return his affection. The sorrow is somewhat undercut, in that this theme is familiar to many readers.

D. H. Lawrence, The Horse Dealer's Daughter

In "The Horse Dealer's Daughter," two lonely people come together after one of them, Mabel, is rescued by the other, Jack, from a suicide attempt. The rescue leads quickly to passion, which leads, just as quickly, to mutual declarations of love.

After the death of Mabel's father, the family farm goes bankrupt because Mabel's brothers are too incompetent to run it successfully. Mabel does not know what to do or where to go and decides her only option is to drown herself in a nearby pond. Dr. Jack Ferguson, a friend of her brothers, happens to be passing by, rescues her, and revives her. In a sense reborn, Mabel's long-suppressed passion is released. Though he is somewhat disconcerted, Jack returns her passion and the story ends with them declaring their love for each other, Mabel confidently, Jack more tentatively.

The theme of "The Horse Dealer's Daughter" is the power of emotional energy suddenly released after years of restraint. Both Mabel and Jack are lonely people in need of a significant relationship, she because she has been her brothers' servant and little else since her parents died, he because his work as a doctor in a poor north England countryside is less than fulfilling. Their union seems both predictable and natural.

Some readers see a subtext at work in the story. It is possible that Mabel plans the entire affair, waiting until a time when she knows the doctor will be passing by the pond before she walks in to drown herself. Jack is strangely drawn to Mabel early in the story in a way that almost suggests she has been bewitching him. This subtext, of course, alters the theme of the story, which now becomes a comment on the power that women have to entrap men when they want or need to do so.

WAR

War is another common subject for works of literature. There are poems and stories that celebrate the courage and honor displayed in a time of war, but, by and large, poets and storytellers write of the horrors of war, of the tragic and futile loss of human life and property.

Wilfred Owen, Futility

Wilfred Owen is one of the best-known World War I poets. In his heartbreaking sonnet, "Futility," he writes of a young soldier, killed on the battlefields of France.

"Move him into the sun," the poem begins, as the speaker makes a futile and desperate attempt to bring the boy back to life, just as the sun woke him from sleep back home. The sun has enormous power, awakening seeds and even "Woke once the clays of a cold star" (line 9). But the sun meets its match on the killing fields of France and can never bring the young soldier back to life.

Owen's theme is that the greatest of war's many evils is its inevitable waste of young life.

Denise Levertov, What Were They Like

In his poem, Owen mourns the loss of the life of a young soldier; in hers, Levertov mourns the civilian victims of war, in the case of this poem, the war in Vietnam.

The format of Levertov's poem is unique. Her poem consists of two stanzas. The first asks a series of six questions, which the second answers. She numbers the questions, which seem innocent and sincere, the questions of someone curious to learn about the customs of the people of Vietnam: Do they love nature? Do they love to laugh? Are they artistically inclined? The answers are blunt, brutal, and direct. It is hard to appreciate the beauty of nature when your children are dying; a burned mouth will not laugh; poetry and song cannot be heard above the screams of those fleeing bombs.

The theme of "What Were They Like" is that the life war destroys is more complex than flesh and blood, including as well the gardens, the art, and the culture a community creates.

Tim O'Brien, The Things They Carried

O'Brien's short story is set during the war in Vietnam. It is about an army platoon, patrolling the jungles of Vietnam and coping with the stress that comes with active duty.

The things these young men carry are both tangible and intangible. They carry the tools of their trade—weapons of every description, radios, explosives, food, maps, medical supplies, compasses. They carry mementos from their loved ones—bibles, letters, and good-luck charms; they carry personal effects ranging from tanning lotion to chewing tobacco. And they carry those intangible things that soldiers carry: fear, responsibility for each other's lives, ghosts, "the weight of memory," and a "silent awe for the terrible power of the things they carried."

The story's central episode is the death of one of the soldiers, Ted Lavender, who is shot when his platoon is on a mission to destroy a tunnel system in Than Khe. The tragedy is devastating to the story's main character, Lieutenant Jimmy Cross, who is already strained with the knowledge that the girl he loves back home may like but will never love him back. Vietnam, of course, compounds the strain. As a gesture of defeat, Cross burns Martha's letters and pictures, even while, subconsciously, he knows he cannot burn the blame he feels for Lavender's death.

Other characters react with mixtures of grief, false bravado, verbosity. In all of their responses to the death of their comrade and to the totality of their experience as soldiers in a foreign country, O'Brien conveys the sense that war is bizarre and aberrant, and forces young men to carry burdens no one should expect them to carry.

Randall Jarrell, The Death of the Ball Turret Gunner

Jarrell's brief, five-line poem is set during the Second World War and describes the gruesome death of a ball turret gunner, killed in action. Ball turret gunners often suffered horrific deaths because they were so exposed to enemy fire. Ball turrets were usually on the underside of high-altitude bombers, so the gunners inside of them were extremely vulnerable to attacking planes.

Despite its brevity, Jarrell's poem accomplishes much. He manages to condemn both war and an absurd foreign policy that leads to war. Using an extended metaphor, he graphically compares the gunner's death to a botched abortion. And he presents the poem as a first-person narration, which heightens his antiwar theme by giving a human voice to one of warfare's most common victims.

Joseph Heller, Catch 22

No novel captures the absurdity of war better than Heller's Catch 22. Published in 1961, Catch 22 has become one of the best-known satiric novels exposing the irrationality of war. The title refers to the loophole (the "catch") that makes it impossible for a soldier to leave military service on the grounds of insanity: If a soldier asks to be excused from battle on the grounds of insanity, he or she is clearly not insane. Upon such twisted logic, the world of Catch 22 revolves. The novel depicts a world overcome by the madness and the unrelenting absurdity of worldwide warfare, and poses this question: How can an ordinary man function in such an extraordinary world?

The ordinary man is John Yossarian, a U.S. Air Force bombardier, stationed on the Island of Pianosa, off the coast of Italy. He abhors the bombing missions he must fly and is baffled by the eccentricity of the officers who serve with him. Throughout the novel, he tries to find ways to understand and cope with the bizarre world in which he must live. He admits himself to the hospital, but there he finds himself next to a patient literally bandaged from head to foot, a patient whom the nurses treat by intravenously draining fluids from his body, then by intravenously dripping the same fluids back into his body. He confides in a fellow officer his fear that people are out to kill him and finds no solace in his friend's logic when the friend reminds him that in a war everyone is trying to kill everyone else. He attends educational sessions where he asks such difficult questions that his superiors forbid him to ask any more questions, then cancel the sessions because no one asks any questions. He tries to appeal to his squadron commander, Major Major, but the Major will never see anyone when he is in his office, only when he is not. He worries about his competence as a bombardier but finds himself decorated and promoted for his incompetence because this is how the Air Force covers up any mistakes it might have made. In this way, with a series of episodes and incidents each one more bizarre than the last, the plot of *Catch 22* unfolds, and Yossarian becomes progressively more alienated, disenchanted, and disillusioned.

His alienation and disillusionment are further compounded by the military's complicity in the money-making schemes of the mess officer, Milo Minderbinder. To Milo, the war is an entrepreneurial opportunity. He gets into the wholesale food business and soon commandeers Air Force fighter planes, newly emblazoned with his company's name, "M&M Enterprises, Fine Fruits and Produce," to pick up and deliver his inventory. He makes a contract with the German government to defend a strategic bridge and a contract with the American government to attack the same bridge, and since the bridge is both attacked and defended, he makes a huge profit. He makes Sicily the world's third-largest exporter of Scotch and is elected mayor of Palermo. He also becomes, by virtue of his amazing business successes, Assistant Governor General of Malta, Vice-Shah of Oran, the Caliph of Baghdad, the Imam of Damascus, and the Sheik of Araby. Typically, Yossarian refuses to do business with Milo, a gesture that impresses Milo, who reasons that anyone who would not steal from his country would not steal from anybody. Yossarian is rather in awe of Milo, until Yossarian has to treat a wounded comrade, only to discover that the morphine is missing, having been appropriated for the greater good of Milo's business dealings. Milo conducts his business with the approval of his superiors who, themselves, make money from his syndicate. In the figure of Milo Minderbinder, Heller satirizes the swashbuckling capitalism that realizes the American dream only for those, like Milo, ready to cut ethical corners.

Religion, with its promise of salvation, hovers around Yossarian throughout the novel but ultimately disappoints him as well. The squadron's spiritual advisor is the ineffectual Chaplain Captain Tappman, whose tongue-twister name reflects his incompetence. Tappman is a sensitive and caring man but these qualities are of no use to him in the world of Pianosa. Tappman is plagued by doubts about his vocation, afraid of men with loud voices, and uncomfortable with any kind of confrontation. Much as he wants to, he cannot effectively meet the spiritual needs of his men because he cannot stand up to his superiors when they usurp his authority, as they do often and in strange ways. Tappman represents the impotence of faith in an absurd universe.

Still, despite the obstacles, Yossarian struggles to do what is right. He tries, to no avail, to reason with his superior officers and to get them to reduce the excessive number of missions he and his fellow pilots and bombardiers must fly. Unlike most of his fellow officers, he treats the hookers who service the squadron like human beings although he almost gets murdered for doing so. He sees the crimes behind Milo's get-rich-quick schemes and refuses to participate in them. He tries to care for his wounded comrades, only to find Milo has stolen the medicine Yossarian needs.

But, in the end, Yossarian is overwhelmed by the omnipresence of the irrational, and he gives up in defeat. He resorts to the only option left to him. He deserts. He runs away to neutral Sweden. Yossarian's roommate, Orr, has already deserted to Sweden by the time Yossarian makes his own decision to do so, and Yossarian comes to realize that Orr, a seemingly inconsequential and nondescript figure throughout the novel, has made the right choice. As his name suggests, Orr (or) offers an alternative to life in an absurd world. Other good men have reasoned that if you can't beat them, join them, and they have become a part of Pianosa's twilight zone, as Yossarian himself almost does when he appears in the nude to accept his medal to protest the increase in the number of missions he is forced to fly. But he reasons, finally, that if you can't beat them, if they are corrupt beyond salvation, it is best to run away from them.

An important theme of *Catch 22* is that war is such an irrational human undertaking that the only thing to do, the right thing to do, is to simply refuse to participate.

Irene Zabytko, Home Soil

A theme of Zabytko's moving short story "Home Soil" is that war goes around and comes around in a never-ending circle of shame and victimization.

The narrator is a veteran of the Second World War. As a Ukrainian, he fought with the Germans to free the Ukraine from Polish and Russian domination. He even wrote "light verse that glorified Hitler as the protector of the free Ukrainian nation." He describes one incident when he pushed a Jewish girl onto a train that would take her to a concentration camp. Every day, the guilt and shame he feels because of his callousness torment him.

The narrator welcomes home his son, returning from a tour of duty in Vietnam. His son appears remote and distant, and at the end of the story he breaks down. He cannot fully articulate his feelings, but clearly his experiences in Vietnam have created within him the same shame and guilt his father still carries with him, in the aftermath of his own Second World War experience. The father comforts the son "the way I saw his mother embrace him when he was afraid to sleep alone."

"Home Soil" is about more than the horror of war. It asks why one war is not enough, why we would subject ourselves to something so awful again and again. It is proof of George Santayana's dictum that those who don't learn from history are condemned to repeat it.

Richard Eberhart, The Fury of Aerial Bombardment

In many ways, Eberhart's sixteen-line World War II poem is typical of antiwar poetry in general. He is saddened by the loss of young life, especially of the friends described in the final quatrain, friends with whom he apparently went to school. He comments on the historical popularity of warfare and wonders if it is not somehow a part of human nature to fight and kill.

What distinguishes Eberhart's poem from other war poems is the intensity with which he introduces God into the whole equation. He poses a question often asked during time of war: How can a compassionate God allow humanity to behave in such a way without visiting his divine justice upon us? Given that technology has advanced so far that the innocent now face the fury of aerial bombardment, may we not expect God finally to "relent" (line 2) and proclaim that enough is enough? Indeed, there is an implied atheism in the theme of the poem, a suggestion that a world wallowing in such violence belongs more to a Satan (the "Beast" of line 12) than to a just God.

NATURE

Observations about nature are common in literature, especially in poetry. Poets often celebrate the beauty of nature, describe the soothing effect nature's beauty has on them, stand in awe of nature's strength and power, and ponder the spiritual implications of nature's apparent order and harmony.

John Keats, To Autumn

In his ode "To Autumn," John Keats describes the sense of tranquility nature gives us when, in the autumn, she is at her richest and most radiant. In the first stanza, he describes with vivid imagery the ripe fruit, the plump gourds and hazel shells, and the late fall flowers, still radiantly blooming. In the second stanza, he writes of the harvest, and personifies autumn as a beautiful farm worker, "Thy hair soft-lifted by the winnowing wind;" (line 14), as she reaps the harvest, rests, and watches "the last oozings" of the cyder press. In the third and final stanza, Keats describes the music of autumn, the gnats mourning the end of summer, the lambs bleating, the soft treble of the red-breast's whistle.

Keats's theme is that when there is perfect harmony within the natural world, there can be, as well, perfect harmony within the human world.

A. J. M. Smith, The Lonely Land

In this poem, Smith celebrates the beauty of the Canadian landscape, specifically, the Ontario lake district, as rendered by Group of Seven artists. Published in 1936, the poem was originally called "Group of Seven" and was, in part, written in praise of the way these painters (the best known include A.Y. Jackson, Tom Thompson, and Lauren Harris) rendered Canada's stark beauty.

The poem praises the beauty of nature through a series of paradoxes. The land is stark and lonely but beautiful and full of natural sounds: a wild duck calling to her mate (lines 12–13); "the lapping of water / on smooth, flat stones" (lines 21–22). The beauty is dissonant (line 24). It is the beauty, described in the famous last lines, "of strength / broken by strength / and still strong" (lines 37–39). Smith's natural world has strength enough in reserve to transcend its own self-destruction.

A main theme of Smith's poem is that nature's beauty is complex and multifaceted. Keats's autumn is appreciated for its tranquility and rich abundance. Smith's lonely land is, by contrast, lean and cold, more eerie than tranquil, but no less beautiful.

Maxine Kumin, Morning Swim

In "Morning Swim," Kumin uses the occasion of an early-morning swim in a lake on a cool misty morning to comment on the connection between the human and natural worlds. The quality of the connections she makes between the two worlds, the human and the natural, are fascinating. It is, in a way, sexual:

I hung my bathrobe on two pegs.
I took the lake between my legs.
(lines 8–9)

It is also spiritual. The rhythm of the swim reminds the narrator of the rhythm of a hymn, specifically of "Abide With Me." She hums the hymn as she swims, and the beat of the tune becomes one with the rhythm of her stroke.

A theme of Kumin's poem is that we can connect on fundamental levels with nature, so much so, in fact, that the line between the human and the natural is blurred. "I was the well," Kumin writes, as the poem comes to an end:

> that fed the lake that met my sea
> in which I sang "Abide With Me."
> (lines 23–24)

Emily Dickinson, I Taste a Liquor

Dickinson celebrates the beauty and the abundance of nature through the words of a narrator who describes how she drinks in the fragrance and the splendor of summer flowers. The effect is literally intoxicating. The metaphor alluded to in the title, of nature as the finest of wine, continues throughout the poem. The narrator is an "Inebriate of Air" (line 5), a "Debauchee of Dew" (line 6), "the little Tippler" (line 15), as she flits among the foxgloves and the bluebells.

Like Keats in his ode "To Autumn," Dickinson highlights nature's apparently inexhaustible supply of fragrance and beauty, which is supremely sensuous without becoming oppressive.

DEATH

The bumper sticker reads "Life is hard and then you die." But as a literary theme, death is rarely an occasion for exasperation and sorrow but more often an opportunity for speculation about the immortality of the human soul.

William Butler Yeats, Sailing to Byzantium and Byzantium

In "Sailing to Byzantium," Yeats writes about his own desire for immortality. He loved Byzantine art and architecture and expresses here his desire to be reincarnated as a Byzantine *object d'art,* specifically a bird carved in gold. He will leave Ireland to the young, he says, and, after his death, his soul will "sail," to Byzantium. There he will continue his role as a poet, prophet, and historian, of Byzantium now, not Ireland.

In a later, related poem, "Byzantium," Yeats imagines he has achieved his goal. His soul has sailed to Byzantium, and now, as the golden bird, "In glory of changeless metal" (line

22), watches other souls arrive, go through the purification ritual, and achieve immortality.

Yeats's theme is that death may be the end of physical life, but it is also an opportunity for spiritual reincarnation.

John Donne, Death Be Not Proud

In this poem, his Holy Sonnet 10, Donne personifies death as essentially a weakling. Many think of you, the poet says, as "Mighty and dreadful" (line 2), but really you are weak and ineffectual. Death is no more than eternal sleep. Everyone dies, so you are hardly special. Your bedfellows are poison, war, and sickness, hardly friends to be proud of. Your ultimate defeat will come, gloriously, on Judgment Day, when "death shall be no more" (line 14).

A theme of Donne's sonnet is that death pales into insignificance in the face of the strength of Christian faith.

William Shakespeare, Poor Soul the Center of My Sinful Earth

In Sonnet 146, one of the last in his famous collection, Shakespeare compares and contrasts the soul to the body. Why, he asks, do we spend so much time and money adorning and obsessing about our bodies when corporal life is so short? Why do we not worry more about our souls? The soul must transcend the body, the poet argues. If the soul feeds upon that which dies, the soul kills death "And Death once dead, there's no more dying then" (line 14).

This sonnet is typically ingenious. Its theme is not merely that the soul survives the body, but that the soul lives off that which kills the body, off Death itself. Like Donne, Shakespeare personifies Death, suggesting that the soul does more than triumph over Death; the soul murders Death.

Dylan Thomas, A Refusal to Mourn the Death by Fire of a Child in London

We would expect our poets to mourn the death of a child, killed during the German blitz of London during the Second World War. Why does Thomas refuse to do so? His answer, which is the essence of his poem, is a curious mix of Christianity and paganism. The pagan part of his answer is that after death we are returned to the earth, which our flesh nourishes. The dead child lies among "The grains beyond age, the dark veins of her mother" (line 20). Yet the opening stanza of the poem suggests the Judgment Day, with its connotations of the resurrection of the soul. Thomas refuses to

mourn the child's death both because we return to our natural state after death and because the soul survives the body.

Emily Dickinson, Because I Could Not Stop for Death

Like many poets, Dickinson asserts that death is not the
end but, instead, a new phase of existence. Like many poets,
she personifies death, but she does so in more positive terms
than other poets, surprisingly praising Death for his "civility"
(line 8). Death "kindly" (line 2) picks the narrator up in his car-
riage and takes her away, accompanied by "Immortality"
(line 4). They journey throughout the day, passing by playing
children, "fields of gazing grain" (line 11), the "setting sun"
(line 12). They arrive at the cemetery but merely pause there
to dispose of the physical body in its coffin (stanza 5), before
they proceed. The soul's journey is not over; death is taking
it "toward eternity" (line 24).

A theme of Dickinson's poem is that death is more release
from life than the end of life because the soul survives
eternally.

FAITH

Many poets and storytellers are interested in the role
faith plays in human life and they often express this interest in their work. They write about the nature and the importance of faith, the process of acquiring faith, the sorrow
of losing, and the joy of recovering their faith in a higher
power.

John Donne, Batter My Heart, Three-Personed God

An Anglican priest, John Donne occasionally expressed
doubts in his poetry about the strength of his commitment to
his God. In his sonnet "Batter My Heart," he writes of the
pull of temptation and fears he is drifting away from God's authority. In the poem, he asks God to batter his heart, to break
him and burn him because if he is broken by the love of God,
he will be made whole again. He asks God to imprison him
because to be imprisoned by God's love is to be set free; he
asks God to ravish him because to be ravished by God's love
is to be rendered chaste.

Donne's sonnet is built around a series of paradoxes. A
paradox is a phrase that seems self-contradictory but, in fact,
makes powerful sense by virtue of its lack of logic. When
Donne asks God to "overthrow" him so that he might "rise
and stand," he seems to be making no sense. But his theme

is that we can only rise and stand when God's love knocks us down, and his use of paradox is an effective way of reinforcing this theme.

Philip Larkin, Church Going

Written in the early 1950s, Larkin's poem poses this question: What is the function of the church in an increasingly secular society?

The narrator of the poem is not "going to church" in the conventional sense of the term. He is on a solitary bike ride, and he stops to visit an empty country church, as, he admits, he often likes to do. This church is nothing special. He takes his tour, makes a modest donation, and asks himself why he bothered stopping, what role does the church play in the modern world, what is the future of English churches?

His answer forms the bulk of the poem: the last five of the poem's seven stanzas. At first, his answer is cynical. Perhaps the better churches will become museums and the ordinary ones barns (stanza 3). Perhaps women, desperate for good luck or for a cure for a cancer, will pay a secret visit to the churchyard (stanza 4). Perhaps a history buff or antique hunter or someone nostalgic for an old-fashioned Christmas will be the last to visit.

However, in the final stanza, the narrator offers a more serious answer. The church will never be obsolete because it will remain a place to come to in the spirit in which the poem's narrator visits this particular church. It is a quiet retreat, a place to think, a place where wisdom can be acquired "If only that so many dead lie round" (line 63).

Larkin's theme might strike the faithful as a half-hearted endorsement of organized religion and the unfaithful as a dubious attempt to justify the role of the church in a society increasingly reluctant to embrace organized religion.

George Herbert, The Collar

Herbert was an Anglican priest, and in this poem he gives voice to the doubts and concerns he had about his vocation.

He starts off angry. He feels that life is passing him by. He is a free man but is bound by his duty to God. He wants to travel, to live the life he led in his youth when he was carefree and hedonistic. He resolves to make up for lost time, to recover "all [his] sigh-blown age / On double pleasures" (lines 19–20). His argument and his anger intensify, until he hears the Lord's voice calling to him, *"Child!"* (line 35), at which point his anger and resentment disappear and he accepts again, willingly, his obligation to God.

The "Caller," then, is God who summons his would-be rebellious priest back into the holy fold. Priests will often say they became priests in answer to a call from God. Herbert spells his title, of course, as "The Collar," a reference to the clerical collar, which is a symbol, at the beginning of the poem, of the stranglehold the poet imagines God has over him. There is even a third pun on the title, in that the narrator also gives vent to his "choler," that is, his anger throughout much of the poem. A theme of Herbert's poem is that God's grace dispels anger and steadies the defiance of the faithful.

Wallace Stevens, Sunday Morning

Poems about faith usually focus on belief in God, and on all of the doubts, triumphs, and challenges that attend a belief in a higher power. Stevens's poem is different. His faith is directed not toward God but toward man and his relationship to the eternal beauty of nature as both the source and the proper focus for human faith.

The poem opens with a description of a woman who is feeling guilty because it is Sunday morning, and she is lounging around enjoying the day, when she should be at church. The poem's narrator defies her guilt. His basic argument, which stretches over most of the poem's eight stanzas and 120 lines, is that human faith is evolving away from conventional Christianity. We began, his argument goes, by worshipping many gods, led by Jove who was divine. Then we progressed to the worship of Christ who is both human and divine. Now it is time to worship, within the context of earthly as opposed to heavenly beauty, that which is wholly human. "Divinity must live within herself" (Stanza II, line 23), the narrator asserts, refuting the argument of the woman who is feeling guilty about neglecting her Christian duties. She can find, "in comforts of the sun" (Stanza II, line 19)—as opposed to comforts of the "Son"—the spiritual fulfillment that she seeks. Indeed, she can find:

> In any balm or beauty of the earth,
> Things to be cherished like the thought of heaven.
> (Stanza II, lines 22–23)

The woman takes a different argumentative tack, stating that she needs the sense of eternity, heaven, and paradise that the Christian faith promises. The narrator counters that nature is, itself, eternal, heavenly, and paradisical. "Death is the mother of beauty" (Stanza V, line 63), the poet states. Nature is a spiritual presence because it dies and is reborn;

it changes. Heaven, in the Christian sense of the term, is, by contrast, static, a nonentity because if it is always the same, always perfect, it is a void. It makes more spiritual sense, the poet argues, to worship the earth than to aspire to heaven (Stanza VI). The sun (Stanza VII) should become the focal point of human worship.

By the end of the poem, the narrator has won the day. The woman accepts the poet's concept of a faith evolving away from a Christian half-man half-god and toward an incarnation that is fully human and natural: "an old chaos of the sun" (Stanza VIII, line 110).

"Sunday Morning" is an essentially pagan poem that reverences the human in complete harmony with the natural.

TIME

Writers are often struck by the transience of time and the brevity of human life. Often in their work, they urge us to make the most of the time available to us. The **carpe diem** or "seize the day" theme, whereby a writer reminds readers that time flies and that life must be lived to the full, is a common one.

Robert Herrick, To the Virgins to Make Much of Time

Herrick's poem is the archetypal *carpe diem* poem. It is an exhortation to young women to enjoy life because "Old time is still a-flying" (line 2). Life is short; if you do not enjoy your salad days, the poet suggests, you will be sorry when you are old and you have lost the energy and the vitality of your youth.

Herrick's general theme is that because time flies, every second, especially the seconds of youth, should be savored. A more specific theme, implied in the title of the poem, the reference to the warm blood of youth (line 10) and the recommendation to "be not coy" (line 13), is that young women should not be too reluctant to surrender their virginity.

A. E. Housman, Loveliest of Trees

In "Loveliest of Trees," A. E. Housman describes a beautiful spring scene, the focus of which is a cherry tree "hung with bloom" (line 2). He is twenty years old and reasons that he has only fifty more springs to appreciate nature's beauty. Since "Fifty springs are little room" (line 9) to admire nature's beauty, he resolves to return to this place in the winter "To see the cherry hung with snow" (line 12). Life is brief, Housman says, and we must appreciate nature's beauty, regardless of the season.

Edna St. Vincent Millay, What Lips My Lips Have Kissed

The narrator of Millay's famous sonnet tries to remember the many loves of her youth. She has trouble remembering the men who turned to her at midnight with a cry (line 8), and she is sorry her memory is failing her because it is all she has left now in her older age. She feels lonely, like a tree in the winter, without its leaves. "I only know," she writes in the last two lines, "that summer sang in me / A little while that in me sings no more."

"What Lips My Lips Have Kissed" is a sad poem about the transience of youth and the loneliness of old age.

Denise Levertov, A Time Past

"A Time Past" is typical of "the golden moment" theme common in poetry. The narrator remembers a perfect fall morning when she was sitting on the steps to her house. Her husband came out of the front door and, overcome by the beautiful day and his sudden presence, she leaped to her feet to tell him how much she loved him. He replied, "I love you too" (line 24). For that moment time seemed to stand still for her, the crickets and the birds fell silent, and golden leaves spun to the ground (lines 24–26).

But time can never stand still. The wooden steps to the house have gone, "replaced with granite" (line 10). The marriage has gone, replaced by memories. "A Time Past" is both a sad and a joyous poem. The joy comes from the realization that such golden moments exist; the sorrow comes from the knowledge that they are transitory.

Metaphor

A **metaphor** is a comparison, the purpose of which is to clarify or intensify the more complex of the objects being compared. When we say that a person is "a real peach" or "a rock" or "a flower child" or "a pain in the neck" or "a space cadet" or a "sweetheart," we are using metaphor to help convey that person's personality or behavior. A **simile** is a type of metaphor that makes the comparison explicit by using either the word "like" or the word "as." Marlene Dietrich used a simile when she sang, in *The Blue Angel,* "men cluster to me <u>like</u> moths around a flame." Another form of metaphor is **personification,** which compares something nonhuman with something that is. When Ralph Hodgson wrote "Time you old gypsy man, / Will you not stay?" he was personifying time as a gypsy, always moving on. A **hyperbole** is a metaphor that bases its comparison on the use of exaggeration. When Al Jolson said of his mother "I'd walk a million miles for one of your smiles," he was using hyperbole to indicate the depth of his affection. **Litotes** is a deliberate use of understatement, usually to create an ironic or satiric effect. When a teacher criticizes her students for not grasping a simple point by saying "this is not rocket science," she is using litotes. **Metonymy** is a specific form of metaphor in which a phrase is understood to represent something more. When the press says the President is "saber rattling," readers understand the use of the metaphor for threatening war. Similarly, a **synecdoche** is the use of a part to represent a whole, as in the expression "lend me a hand." In literature, a metaphor can develop character, clarify theme, and intensify symbolism.

METAPHOR AND CHARACTER

A metaphor can help develop a character and clarify a character's actions and motivation.

William Shakespeare, That Time of Year Thou Mayest in Me Behold

The narrator of this Shakespeare sonnet is an old man with not a lot of time left to live. He wants his partner to love him all the more strongly because he will be leaving her so soon. To stress his point, he compares himself to late autumn. There are only a few "yellow leaves" (line 2) left upon the tree of his life. He compares himself to the day's twilight, living just before the darkness of night falls (lines 5–8). He compares himself to a fire that has burned down to its embers (lines 9–12).

The metaphors Shakespeare uses here, comparing the seasons of our lives to the seasons of the year and the stage of our lives to the time of the day, are ones poets commonly use.

Stevie Smith, Not Waving but Drowning

A wave of the hand is an interesting metaphor. It can represent, among other things, a friendly greeting or a plea for help.

Stevie Smith uses this metaphor in her poem "Not Waving but Drowning" to make a comment on our indifference to the suffering of our fellow man. The narrator is swimming in the ocean and his waves are mistaken for friendly waves, when they are, in fact, pleas for help from a drowning man. The cold water of the ocean becomes a metaphor for life. "I was much too far out all my life" (line 11), the narrator says, referring more to his emotional state than his ocean swim. The narrator needs emotional support but those who see his wave prefer to interpret it as a casual sign of friendship, rather than a cry for help. A cry for help would require the effort of emotional support we prefer to withhold.

James Joyce, Clay

"Clay" is the story of Maria, a kitchen maid who works in a Dublin laundry. The story is set on Halloween and tells of Maria's visit to her brother Joe's house for a Halloween party. She arrives at the party and is disappointed to discover she has left on the tram the plum cake she wanted to contribute. She plays a fortune-telling game and, blindfolded, puts her hands on a prayer book, indicating a future life in the Church. She tries to make peace between her feuding brothers but fails. She sings a song but forgets the second verse. The story ends.

The plot of the story seems rather inconsequential, as does the story's main character. But a closer reading reveals Joyce's interesting use of metaphor, particularly personification. Physically Maria resembles a fairy-tale witch, with her long nose and pointed chin, which almost meet when she laughs. But her name is Maria and she is described as "proper mother," which suggests the Virgin Mary. She sets out on Halloween night like a good witch, but, like a good Catholic, she sets her alarm so she can be up early enough for All Saints' Day Mass. She is known as a peacemaker at work because she can always settle a quarrel between her co-workers. Yet she cannot make the peace between her two brothers. She is neat, precise, and orderly in all things, yet she leaves her plum cake on the tram. She chooses the prayer book during the fortune-telling game but, unbeknownst to her, she first chooses a saucer full of clay, representing death—the saucer was not supposed to be part of the game and the embarrassed hosts throw it away before she is aware of what she has chosen.

A common interpretation of this story is that Maria is a personification of Ireland itself. The Ireland Joyce loved and hated was a country that, in Joyce's opinion, shared many of the characteristics Joyce gives to Maria. It was ruled by a Church that was autocratic and corrupt, traits reflected in Maria's dual identity of Madonna and witch. Maria's choice of the clay followed by the prayer book has similar symbolic significance, as does the setting: the eve of Allhallows is followed by All Saints Day. Like Maria, Ireland tries to make peace between its warring factions, but, like Maria who cannot make peace between her brothers, it continues to fail to do so. Some critics suggest that her loss of her plum cake symbolizes the theft of Ireland by the British, since the gentleman who talks to her on the tram and flusters her into forgetting her cake rather resembles a British colonel. Others suggest her forgetfulness when singing "I Dreamt that I Dwelt" mirrors the Irish tendency to forget the significance of its own past.

Certainly, Maria's character is metaphorical. The precise nature of the significance of the metaphor is, like most of Joyce's work, open to interpretation, though the schizophrenic attitude towards Ireland, implicit in "Clay," is often evident in Joyce's work.

John Donne, The Flea

The narrator of "The Flea" is defined by the ingenious if desperate metaphor that he uses to try to persuade a young woman to have sex with him.

"Mark but this flea" the narrator tells his date as the poem opens, "and mark in this / How little that which thou deny'st me is" (lines 1–2). She is denying him sex on the grounds that she refuses to sacrifice her honor. He is claiming that, because a flea has already bitten both of them, they have had sex already because their blood is intermingled in the body of the flea. The woman kills the flea and, in triumph, claims that both she and the narrator are alive and not even weakened by the flea's death, so that his argument that they live in the body of the flea is clearly nonsense. The narrator agrees, saying that the flea's death did not weaken them. It follows, therefore, that she will lose the same amount of honor when she yields to him as "this flea's death took life from thee" (line 27). In other words, she will lose no honor by having sex with the narrator.

The metaphor reveals the narrator to be a clever debater who skillfully maneuvers his date into a position where she has to consider the possibility that the honor she is protecting is worth less than she had thought. But it also reveals him to be a rogue, who will play curious mind games to persuade a young woman to sleep with him.

METAPHOR AND THEME

In addition to helping establish character, a metaphor can intensify the theme of a literary work.

John Donne, A Valediction: Forbidding Mourning

In "A Valediction: Forbidding Mourning," Donne uses a striking metaphor to intensify the theme of the poem. Donne compares the love he has for his wife with the love other couples share and pronounces the love he shares with his wife superior because it is spiritual as much as it is physical. The poet is leaving the country on business and urges his wife not to mourn his absence. Because of their spiritual bond, he says, wherever he goes, he takes her with him. He compares the two of them to the two feet of a mathematical compass. Her soul is "the fixed foot" (line 26) and "leans and harkens after" the other foot when it goes away. Together, they form a circle, a symbol of both perfection and a wedding band. They come together again when the wandering foot returns:

Thy firmness makes my circle just,
And makes me end where I begun.
(lines 35–36)

Ingenious, elaborate metaphors such as the one Donne uses in "A Valediction: Forbidding Mourning" are called **conceits.**

W. S. Merwin, Separation

A theme of Merwin's very brief poem is that people in love find it hard to be apart. He employs a very effective simile to amplify this theme. "Your absence has gone through me," the poet says to his partner, "Like thread through a needle. / Everything I do is stitched with its color" (entire poem). The simile suggests how the poet is torn apart by his friend's absence, how everything he does now involves some attempt to stitch his life back together.

John Keats, On First Looking into Chapman's Homer

An important theme of Keats's sonnet is the joy of discovery. Specifically, the poet writes of his own joy at discovering the works of Homer, in the George Chapman translation. Reading Homer opened up a whole new world to the young poet. He compares his experience to the feelings an astronomer must have when he or she discovers a new planet and to the awe Cortez must have experienced when he first saw the Pacific Ocean from the heights of Darien in Panama. (Apparently, it was actually Balboa who saw the Pacific from Darien—Keats's recollection of his history lessons is off.) These two metaphors for the joy of discovery augment the poet's own sense of wonder that he experienced reading *The Iliad* for the first time.

Edgar Allan Poe, The Masque of the Red Death

The central metaphor in Poe's story helps define the character of the protagonist, Prince Prospero. The red death is a deadly plague that has gripped the kingdom Prospero rules. His response to the plague is to run away and hide. Terrified of suffering and dying, he abandons his people and, with his closest friends, advisors, and protectors, he retires to the seclusion of his magnificent country palace. There he throws lavish parties and revels in the knowledge that he has cheated death by escaping from the plague. But, of course, he has not. Among the party guests, at the most elaborate masque the Prince has hosted, appears the red death, personified as tall and gaunt, "and shrouded from head to foot in the habiliments of the grave." One by one, beginning with the Prince himself, the party guests drop to the floor and die.

The red death is a multidimensional metaphor. It is a metaphor for deathly fear from which we cannot run but must confront. It reminds us that wealth and privilege do not grant immunity from reality. And it is a metaphor, in the form of a personification, for death from which there is ultimately no escape.

William Shakespeare, My Mistress's Eyes Are Nothing Like the Sun

In this sonnet, Shakespeare uses reverse metaphors to describe and compliment the object of his desire and affections. Common similes and metaphors have become clichés: her eyes are like the sun; her lips are as red as coral; roses are in her cheeks. What Shakespeare does here is to proclaim that his mistress's eyes are "nothing like the sun" (line 1), that roses are not in her cheeks (line 6), that her voice is not like music (line 9). But there is a method to his apparent tactlessness. He is actually praising his mistress by accentuating her uniqueness. The poet's inability to find suitable metaphors to define her character and beauty accentuates his view that his love is "as rare / As any she belied with false compare" (lines 13–14).

METAPHOR AND SYMBOLISM

A metaphor is a comparison between two objects. A symbol is somewhat similar: It is an object, a character, or an event that reverberates with suggestions and implications beyond its literal meaning. Sometimes a writer will augment a metaphor by ascribing symbolic connotations to one of the objects that comprise the comparison.

William Blake, A Poison Tree

Blake's poem is about anger that flourishes because it goes unexpressed and ultimately becomes poisonous. This anger is, metaphorically, a tree that is watered by anger's tears and fed by anger's "soft deceitful wiles" (line 8). The anger tree thrives and bears a bright shiny apple. The victim of the poet's anger sees the apple, steals it, eats it, and:

> In the morning glad I see
> My foe outstretch'd beneath the tree.
> (lines 15–16)

The poisonous apple has, of course, a long symbolic history, traditionally associated, as it is, with Satan's temptation of Eve. In fairy tales and fables it is, more often than not, a poisonous apple the wicked witch gives to the beautiful princess to put her into a coma. Blake's apple continues the tradition. Fed and watered by hate and anger, the sweet fruit of the apple is corrupted into a poison. The symbolism intensifies Blake's metaphor and the theme of the destructive power of anger, which the metaphor helps to convey.

Robert Frost, Desert Places

In "Desert Places," Frost describes a winter desert, a lonely, snow-covered field that even the animals have abandoned. He compares this desert place to others, "on stars where no human race is" (line 14). The setting should be frightening, redolent as it is with an overwhelming sense of nothingness. But the poet is not frightened by any natural desert. Rather, it is the desert places within his own heart that genuinely scare him.

"Desert Places" is about the pain of human loneliness. Frost uses the natural world as a symbol and a metaphor to convey the depth of the alienation and loneliness the poem's narrator is experiencing.

Emily Dickinson, There's a Certain Slant of Light

In her complex poem "There's a Certain Slant of Light," Emily Dickinson identifies the "slant of light" on a winter afternoon as "the Seal Despair." The metaphor is intriguing. Despair is unpleasant but transitory, and when we recover from despair, we feel renewed. "When it goes," Dickinson writes, "tis like the Distance / On the look of Death—" (lines 15–16).

Some critics feel the "slant of light" has additional symbolic connotations because of the poem's religious context. The light "oppresses, like the Heft / Of Cathedral Tunes" (lines 3–4). It gives us a "heavenly Hurt" (line 5). Some readers feel the slant of light symbolizes the immortality of the soul. Death brings despair but the soul's immortality transcends that despair. The series of paradoxes around which the poem is built—the heft of cathedral tunes, heavenly hurt, the seal despair, an imperial affliction—convey the sorrow of death countermanded by the triumph of the human soul.

Imagery

In literature, an image is a word picture—a phrase, a sentence, or a line—that enhances readers' appreciation of the figurative more than the literal meaning of a poem, story, or play. In other words, writers use imagery to help their readers get a better *sense* of what the writer is trying to communicate. I use the word "sense" instead of "understanding" because an image is sensual, in that it arouses in readers one or more of the five senses. Through the use of an effective image, a writer can help us see or hear or taste or touch or smell what it is he or she is describing. When the narrator of Diane Ackerman's poem "Beija Flor" says that when her lover kisses her "sunset pours molasses down my spine / and, in my hips, the green wings of the jungle flutter" (lines 13–14), she uses vivid images to help convey the sensual pleasure she is experiencing. Imagery can advance the plot of a story, define character, animate setting, and clarify theme.

IMAGERY AND PLOT

Imagery is associated with the artistry of a literary work; plot more with its structure and literal meaning. Yet imagery can signal the direction a plot will take.

Ambrose Bierce, An Occurrence at Owl Creek Bridge

The plot of Ambrose Bierce's American Civil War story, "An Occurrence at Owl Creek Bridge," concerns a Confederate Southern farmer, Peyton Farquar, who is about to be hanged for blowing up a bridge of strategic importance to the enemy. The rope, suspended from the side of Owl Creek Bridge, snaps with Farquar's weight, and he escapes. He makes his way onto shore, dodging Federal bullets. He struggles through the woods, and eventually makes his way back home. But when he is about to embrace his wife, he feels a jolt to his neck. The story ends with a stark description of Farquar hanging from the Owl Creek Bridge. His escape had been a deathbed fantasy.

It is the imagery Bierce uses that first alerts us to the unreality of Farquar's experience. Bierce describes a man whose senses have been honed to supernatural levels. As Farquar emerges from the water and enters the forest, he can see "the brilliant-bodied flies, the gray spiders stretching their webs from twig to twig." He notes "the prismatic colors in all the dewdrops upon a million blades of grass." He hears the "audible music" of the "humming of the gnats that danced above the eddies of the stream, the beating of the dragon-flies' wings, the strokes of the water-spiders' legs." Throughout Farquar's escape fantasy, Bierce uses similar vivid imagery to reflect the perceptions of a man whose senses have been heightened to supernatural levels as he experiences the moment of his own death.

Readers realize, in retrospect, that this imagery signaled the direction the plot was taking. Farquar's escape could not be real because his powers of perception, reflected in Bierce's striking images, were far too acute to be normal. In fact, those images suggested the sharpened sense of sight and sound Bierce imagines a man might experience at the moment of his death.

A. D. Hope, Imperial Adam

Imagery also helps to transmit the plot of Hope's poem "Imperial Adam." The plot concerns the creation of Eve from one of Adam's ribs and the consequences of this creation. Eve tempts Adam with the fruit of the forbidden tree and thereby releases his lust. They couple, Eve becomes pregnant, and gives birth to Cain, who will eventually murder his own brother, Abel. The poem ends dramatically with a description of Cain's birth.

The imagery conveys the beauty of Eden with its ripe fruit trees "drooping their golden breasts" (line 13) while the dew on the grass "winked crisp and fresh" (line 16). The imagery creates a most vivid picture of Adam and Eve coupling, and Eve in the act of birth surrounded by "the first gentle midwives of mankind" (line 35), who are the animals of Eden, many also about to give birth. The imagery intensifies the shock of the poem's ending:

Between her legs a pigmy face appear,
And the first murderer lay upon the earth.
(lines 43–44).

IMAGERY AND CHARACTER

Imagery can also be used to help readers visualize a character whom a writer is describing.

Diane Ackerman, Beija Flor

The narrator of Ackerman's poem defines her romantic and sensuous nature through the catalogue of imagery she uses to describe how she feels when her lover kisses her. The poem is fifty-four lines long and contains sixteen different images, each more sensuous than the last. The images brilliantly capture the sensation of a lover's kiss. The images are drawn from the sounds of jungle animals, from the rivers, the rain, the sunset, the moon, coca trees, exotic birds and flowers, and butterflies. These images create an accumulated impression of unmatched beauty and a picture of a woman almost overwhelmed by the sensual pleasure she is experiencing on many different levels.

Lord Byron, She Walks in Beauty

"She Walks in Beauty" is a good example of the use of imagery to describe physical appearance. The poem describes the beautiful wife of Byron's cousin. Byron first met her in June of 1814, and wrote the poem almost immediately thereafter. She was in mourning and wore a black dress, covered in spangles.

The imagery Byron uses helps readers see a striking dark woman in a black, glowing dress. She is like the night "of cloudless climes, and starry skies" (line 2). Her hair "waves in every raven tress" then "lightens o'er her face" (lines 9–10). The innocent face framed by the raven hair parallels the mellow light the stars emit, amid the black night. The imagery in the first two stanzas prepares readers for the impression conveyed in the final stanza of the woman's winning smile, eloquent demeanor, and gentle heart.

James Joyce, The Dead

The main character of Joyce's story, "The Dead," is Gabriel Conroy, a middle-aged university professor who is emotionally estranged from his family. The imagery in the story helps to convey Gabriel's isolation.

The story is set in Dublin, early in the twentieth century, on the night of Gabriel's aunts' annual Christmas party. Gabriel appears to be an extrovert, as he chats up the kitchen maid, ceremoniously carves the turkey, dances with a colleague, and gives the after-dinner speech. In reality, he is insecure. His thoughts, after he has several rather awkward encounters with other characters and before his speech, reveal a self-conscious and embittered man who hides his insecurity behind a mask of self-assertiveness. The most profound of these encounters is with his own wife, Gretta. She is distracted after the party and Gabriel asks her why. She explains that a song she heard at the party reminded her of a former boyfriend. Gabriel is annoyed and, typically, makes a sarcastic remark. He is silenced when Gretta tells him Michael is dead and that she thinks he died for love of her. She breaks down and cries. Confronted with his wife's raw emotion, Gabriel's eyes begin to open. He realizes his wife does not really love him, nor does he truly love her. He realizes his solicitude towards his aunts is insincere. He realizes he is not the self-possessed and successful man he tries to appear to be. He understands his self-centeredness and begins to realize that no man is an island.

Snow imagery dominates the story and helps to reveal Gabriel's personality and his change in outlook with which the story concludes. Early in the story, the snow is Gabriel's enemy. He "vigorously" scrapes it from his boots; he shuns it when he looks out of his aunts' window. Back at the hotel, after his wife has told him the story of Michael Furey, he gazes out the window again and notices that snow is falling. But now the snow suggests Gabriel's need to be a part of his world, not separate from it. The snow is everywhere. It is falling all over the country, into the ocean, onto the churchyard where Michael Furey is buried. There is no escaping the snow. There is no escaping from the needs and demands of spouses, family, and friends who need our sympathy and compassion more than they want our irony and sarcasm.

Ben Jonson, Still to be Neat

In the first stanza of "Still to be Neat," Jonson describes a woman who is concealing something—her age, perhaps, or a plain face—behind fancy clothing, powder, and perfume. The poet disapproves of such concealment, suggesting, as it does, that "All is not sweet, all is not sound" (line 6). To accentuate his disapproval, he presents, in the second and final stanza, a contrasting image: a woman whose face "makes simplicity a grace" (line 8), whose hair is "free" (line 9), whose clothes are "loosely flowing" (line 9).

The poet, then, establishes an aspect of the character of the woman in the first stanza through the use of the contrasting imagery in the second stanza, which describes his own ideal. The free and natural appearance of the ideal woman of the second stanza exaggerates the rather arrogant and unnatural demeanor of the real woman in the first.

IMAGERY AND SETTING

Imagery is a very important literary device for establishing setting. Writers want their readers to be able to visualize the place where the action of their poem or story takes place, to hear its sounds, and absorb its ambience. Through the effective use of imagery, writers can help give readers a sense of place.

Dylan Thomas, Fern Hill

Fern Hill was the name of the Welsh farmhouse where Thomas spent his boyhood summers. Thomas immortalizes the farm in his poem. His use of imagery creates an indelible picture in the reader's mind of a boy in tune with nature, as he enjoys the freedom of his summer holidays. At his command, Thomas writes, the trees on the farm "Trail with daisies and barley / Down the rivers of the windfall light" (lines 8–9). The "foxes on the hills barked clear and cold" (line 16). The sun seemed to set the grass on fire. Fern Hill is utopia, quite literally, as Thomas makes clear in the fourth stanza of this six-stanza poem, the Garden of Eden.

Thomas writes the poem from the perspective of an adult who knows he cannot turn back the hands of time and relive his past. He knows now time held him "green and dying" (line 53) even during those carefree days on Fern Hill. But the focus of the poem is on the boy's sense of community with all *living* things, as the poem's imagery makes clear.

Indeed, "Fern Hill" is a feast of imagery. In the word picture Thomas paints, readers see the young boy at play on his farm, hear the songs of the owls and the night-jars, and sense the pastoral innocence of the poem's setting.

Evelyn Waugh, Brideshead Revisited

Brideshead Revisited is set primarily in England, between about 1923 and 1941. Brideshead is the name of a large and beautiful country home in Wiltshire and is the focal point for the setting of Waugh's novel. The home is owned by the Flytes, a prominent English Catholic family.

Into the world of the Flytes enters Charles Ryder, the narrator of the novel, who meets Sebastian Flyte at Oxford. They become close friends and lead a rather dissolute life together as undergraduates. Charles eventually moves on, but Se-

bastian becomes an alcoholic and winds up working as a jan-
itor in a Catholic monastery in Morocco. Charles becomes a
landscape painter and on a return voyage from Latin America reencounters Julia Flyte, Sebastian's sister. They fall in
love. They divorce their respective spouses and live together at Brideshead until Julia's other brother, the devout Bridey,
arrives and voices his disapproval. Julia, aware she has been
so untrue to her faith, leaves Charles. War breaks out and
Charles becomes a soldier. He should be desperately unhappy: He is alone, he has lost his friends, and war is rag-
ing. However, he is happy because he has followed the lead
of the Flytes, converted to Catholicism, and found the spiritual strength he needs to survive in an abrasive world.

Yet *Brideshead Revisited* is more than a novel about the
power of faith to influence human life. It is also about the decline of a social order Waugh reverenced. Specifically, Waugh
mourns the decline in influence of the English aristocracy
and the concomitant rise of the middle and working classes,
which, to Waugh, meant that an order and stability was
being sacrificed in the name of a perverted form of democ-
racy. Waugh's imagery reflects his view of a stable social
order beginning to fall apart.

The dominant image and symbol in the novel is the
baroque stately manor, the Flyte home, Brideshead. When
Charles first sees the home he is immediately entranced. It
becomes an oasis to him, a home away from his own home,
which is presided over by his eccentric father. In its pastoral
setting, at the source of the Bride River in the beautiful English countryside, Brideshead is imposing, solid, and archi-
tecturally significant. It is an embodiment of the strength of
the English Catholic tradition in England. But by the end of
the novel, war has broken out and the government has
turned Brideshead into an army barracks. In fact, Charles,
now a middle-aged officer, is stationed there and the house
triggers the memories that form the plot of the novel.

The image of stately Brideshead transformed into an army
barracks becomes a microcosm of Waugh's vision of the social decay of his country. Brideshead's magnificent walls and
fireplaces are covered, the office and the parlor have deteri-
orated, the tapestries are threatened. The beautiful and or-
nate fountain, beside which Charles and Sebastian and later
Charles and Julia once sat, is empty of water and a recepta-
cle now for the soldiers' cigarette butts and garbage. The
Chapel is closed, but, significantly, it is essentially unchanged
and the art-nouveau lamp still nurses a small red flame. Here
is the final image in the novel. England's social structure
might be collapsing, the world might be at war, the Flytes

have, as their name suggests they would, died or scattered themselves around the world, but faith survives it all.

Marge Piercy, Wellfleet Sabbath

Wellfleet is a seaside town close to the northern tip of Cape Cod in Massachusetts. Piercy's imagery compels the reader to see the beauty of Wellfleet at dusk one summer Sunday. "The breast of the bay is softly feathered / dove grey" (lines 2–3). The moon becomes "a copper / balloon just sailing free" (lines 7–8). The ocean "stretches its muscles in the deep, / purrs and rolls over" (lines 11—12). Her images are precise and striking and help readers share the poet's wonder at being confronted by nature's beauty. To the poet, nature's beauty verifies a divine presence. As the poem ends, Piercy imagines the arrival of the Shekinah (line 16), which, in the Jewish faith, is the female aspect of the godhead.

IMAGERY AND THEME

Imagery can be used to underscore the theme of a poem. Indeed, between 1912 and 1917, there was a group of poets who called themselves **imagists,** and their aim was to write poetry that accented imagery or, their preferred term **imagism,** to communicate the poem's meaning. The imagists were influenced by the Japanese **haiku,** a brief poem, consisting of a single image. A Japanese haiku consists of three lines of five, seven, and five syllables, respectively:

> Fir trees hang pine cones.
> Winter winds freeze autumn leaves.
> Pine cones in warm snow.

English haiku writers tend to deviate from this rigid structure while still producing a single-image poem.

William Carlos Williams, The Red Wheelbarrow

Williams's brief, fifteen-word poem presents a single image of a red wheelbarrow, glazed with rainwater, beside a flock of white chickens. The image is simple and direct. Yet the poet asserts that "so much depends" (lines 1–2) upon this single image, suggesting, perhaps, that its simplicity and directness is its primary virtue, that the simple and direct is exactly what we should observe most closely. The poem consists of one sentence but Williams does not arrange the words on the page in the way he would a sentence. He forces us to notice the words and, implicitly, urges us to view reality from a fresh perspective. A theme of the poem is that there is pure beauty in simplicity and the single image helps to convey this theme.

Ezra Pound, In a Station of the Metro

Ezra Pound was a leading exponent of the Imagist school. His haiku, "In a Station of the Metro" consists of fourteen words:

> The apparition of these faces in the crowd,
> Petals on a wet, black bough.

The poem is a single image of faces in a crowded metro station. The faces are compared to petals, which have dropped onto the black bough of a tree after a rain. This connection between the human world and the natural world is typical of the haiku genre. This theme—that human and natural worlds are inextricably connected—is established through the single image Pound presents.

Symbolism

A symbol is an element within a literary work, an element that has more than a literal meaning. In fact, some symbols, known as **universal** or **cultural symbols,** do not require the context of literature to communicate their nonliteral meaning. We wave our country's flag at an international sporting event and all recognize the flag as a symbol of support and national pride. If we send a dozen long-stem red roses to someone, the recipient understands the roses as a symbol of our affection. A **contextual symbol** is one that has nonliteral meaning only within the context of the work of art in which it is found. The farmer in Breughel's painting "Landscape with the Fall of Icarus" is a contextual symbol of human indifference, while Icarus himself (who tried to fly to the sun but fell to his death when his wax wings melted) is a universal symbol of the energy of the human spirit. Anything—any object or element of nature—within a work of literature can have symbolic overtones. Even a character in a work of literature might represent or symbolize something that transcends the character's literal role or function in the story.

OBJECTS AS SYMBOLS

Any object in a work of literature can have symbolic overtones. A handgun might be a phallic symbol, a coffee spoon might symbolize dull routine, a broken clock might symbolize death.

Emily Dickinson, My Life Had Stood a Loaded Gun

Dickinson's poem is narrated from the point of view of a loaded gun that accompanies its owner into the woods when, together, they go hunting. At night the loaded gun vigilantly protects its master. They live together, even sleep together, the hunter and his loyal gun, partners but with one key difference. The hunter has a greater power: He has not only the ability to kill but also, unlike the loaded gun, the power to die (lines 23–24).

The gun becomes, at the end of the poem, a strikingly original symbol of the immortality of the soul. Paradoxically, the hunter will live longer than his gun because the gun merely kills; it does not have the human ability to die and achieve immortality.

Other readers interpret the symbolism of the loaded gun differently. Some critics have suggested the loaded gun symbolizes Dickinson's ability as a poet. The hunter is the poet herself, occasionally killing with the weapon of her talent, while protecting her owner from the outside world. Inevitably, Freudian critics see the gun as a phallic symbol, although the plot of the poem seems incapable of sustaining such a reading. Moreover, the use of a gun as a phallic symbol is a cliché a poet of Dickinson's ability would avoid. The use of the impotence of a loaded gun to accent and symbolize the potency of the human soul is more characteristic of the bold use of symbolism that is a hallmark of Dickinson's work.

Sylvia Plath, Mirror

Plath's poem is narrated from the point of view of a mirror. The mirror tells us how, day after day, it watches a woman gaze into its glass and fret as she observes herself aging. The mirror itself is indifferent to the woman's despair. Ageless itself, it dispassionately watches its owner as she worries about the lines that accumulate upon her face as the years pass. The mirror is a symbol of human vanity. Plath satirizes our obsession with the loss of our youth. The woman is a completely authentic character, an icon of our youth-obsessed culture. She displays her acute anxiety about what poet Irving Layton describes as "the unmistakable lousiness of growing old" ("Keine Lazarovitch").

John Keats, Ode on a Grecian Urn

The Grecian urn in Keats's famous ode is a symbol of the harmony of life, of the integral relationship between the real and the imagined, the beautiful and the true. That which is true is also beautiful; that which is beautiful is true.

The poet studies the paintings on a Grecian urn and is struck by the realization that art freezes time. The young woman and the young man who is pursuing her will never grow old and die: "For ever wilt thou love," he says to the young man, "and she be fair!" (line 20). This, he thinks, is paradise. But when he sees another painting on the urn, depicting sacrifice and death, the poet realizes that even a work of art reminds us of the impermanence of life. Art is beautiful, but it is also true. The urn "dost tease us out of thought" (line 44) by promising a pastoral and eternal world that does not really exist. In the end, the urn is "a friend to man" (line 48) because it reminds us that beauty reflects truth and in truth there is beauty. The symbolism of the Grecian urn is established in the poem's famous last lines:

> "Beauty is truth, truth beauty,"—that is all
>   Ye know on earth, and all ye need to know.
> (lines 49–50)

NATURAL SYMBOLS

Writers frequently use as symbols elements within the natural world. Blake's tiger (see Chapter 2), for example, symbolizes nature's power and energy; Coleridge's albatross in "The Rime of the Ancient Mariner" (see Chapter 2) symbolizes the sanctity of nature against which man must not sin; the lake in Maxine Kumin's poem "Morning Swim" (see Chapter 8) is a symbol of the intimate physical link between the human and natural worlds.

Robert Frost, Fire and Ice

Fire symbolizes excessive passion in Frost's brief, eight-line poem, while ice symbolizes hatred. One of these emotions with which Frost associates these two natural forces will, the poet warns, lead to the destruction of the world.

Emily Dickinson, I Heard a Fly Buzz

Dickinson uses a fly as a symbol in her poem "I Heard a Fly Buzz." At the moment of her death, the narrator of the poem hears a fly buzz. The occasion is solemn. The narrator has made her will, "Signed away / What portion of me be / Assignable" (lines 9–11). Now she is dying and her family has gathered beside her bed. As her death comes, "There interposed a Fly"—(line 12); she hears the fly buzz:

> And then the Windows failed—and then
> I could not see to see—
> (lines 15–16)

The fly is symbolic, though readers cannot agree on what the fly symbolizes. Some readers feel it represents Satan, because we associate flies with filth and germs, and therefore

suggests the speaker has not made it to heaven. Other readers feel the fly symbolizes the insignificance of death because
it is such a common household pest. Its presence in the room
undercuts the solemnity of the occasion while it reminds us
that death is an everyday occurrence. Still other readers feel
the fly symbolizes the immortality of the soul, buzzing on
even after the body has died.

Dickinson's poem illustrates the versatility of symbolism.
A symbol can push a literary work in several different directions at once. The reader decides the direction in which symbolism pushes meaning.

William Blake, The Sick Rose

Blake describes a rose whose young and fragile beauty is
destroyed by a worm. In broad terms, the rose symbolizes
innocence and the worm, the corrupting force that destroys
the innocence of youth. In more specific terms, the worm is
a phallic symbol and the poem is about the loss of virginity.
Indeed, "The Sick Rose" comes close to being a poem about
the atrocity of rape.

Dylan Thomas, The Force that through the Green Fuse

The "force" is Thomas's symbol of the connectedness between the human and the natural worlds. The same force
that brings life to flowers, brings life to me, Thomas writes.
The same force that destroys nature—"blasts the roots of
trees" (line 3)—also destroys me (line 4). We may not communicate with nature on a verbal level, but we are united by
a shared force that is both life-giving and death-bearing. The
worm that appears at the very end of the poem (line 16) is
both phallic, and, hence, a symbol of life and parasitic, and,
hence, a symbol of death.

John Steinbeck, The Chrysanthemums

Steinbeck's story is about a childless farmer's wife, Eliza
Allen, who spends much of her days growing and tending to
the fabulous chrysanthemums, which are the pride of her
garden. Her husband teases her, threatening to put her
"planters hands" to work in the apple orchard, a prospect
that actually pleases Eliza much more than it dismays her. A
traveling tinker arrives at the Allen ranch in the Salinas Valley and lavishes praise on Eliza's flowers. Flattered, Eliza
pays him to fix one of her pots. Eliza is strangely drawn to
him, to his itinerant lifestyle and freedom. She reaches out to

touch him. She gives him some cuttings and instructions on how to grow chrysanthemums as beautiful as hers. On the way into town, later that day, Eliza notices her cuttings on the road and realizes the tinker had praised her work only to get the commission.

The chrysanthemums might symbolize Eliza's frustrated maternity and frustrated sexuality. She has abundant energy and a nurturing personality, which her husband does nothing to praise or encourage. She is childless but far from frigid. She is intrigued by her husband's suggestion that she could do more of the man's work around the farm, even though the suggestion was made in jest. She is aroused by the tinker's presence and, metaphorically, hints at her frustrated sexual desire. The chrysanthemums symbolize Eliza's creative potential, which is stifled by a society that denies women sexual and professional liberation.

RELIGIOUS SYMBOLS

Religious symbolism is used widely in literature. Usually, a religious symbol will be used to suggest the need for faith or a crisis of faith a main character is suffering.

James Joyce, Araby

In Joyce's story "Araby," a young adolescent boy experiences his first case of puppy love. The object of his affection is the older sister of his friend, Mangan. He stalks her, and finally works up the courage to speak to her, promising to bring her a present from the fair (called Araby), which he will be attending. But he arrives at the fair late, and he overhears a shop girl flirting inanely with two young men. The experience destroys his idealist view of love, and crushes the illusion of his love for Mangan's sister. "Araby" is a typical "loss of innocence" story. The boy, who is the first-person narrator (see Chapter 6) of the story, learns that Arabian night fantasies of flawless women perched upon pedestals might exist in romance novels but not in real life.

On a symbolic level, the boy learns something else, as well. He learns that in his native Ireland, the Church is a shell of its former self. The Catholic Church is supposed to satisfy the spiritual needs of its congregation, but it has abrogated that responsibility.

Throughout the story, the author makes reference to many religious objects and traditions. In the first paragraph of the story, Joyce describes a central apple tree and a rusty bicycle pump in the boy's yard, symbolizing a corrupt Garden of

Eden and the loss of innocence the boy will experience. The former tenant of the house was a priest, and the house still contains some of the priest's religious books, but they are dog-eared and faded. The boy imagines that he bears a chalice, the cup that holds the communion wine, "safely through a throng of foes." Mangan's sister turns a bracelet made of silver, a symbol of Judas's betrayal of Christ, around her wrist while she talks to the boy. When the boy finally arrives at Araby, he recognizes "a silence like that which pervades a church after a service." He hears the sound of falling coins, reminiscent of the biblical story of the money changers in the temple.

"Araby" is, on the surface, the story of a young boy's unfulfilled quest for romantic love. Symbolically, it is a story of his unfulfilled quest for a true faith. His quest is unfulfilled because the Church has been corrupted by material concerns, and has, in fact, betrayed its flock. The chalice, symbolically the Holy Grail, has not been found. Except for the sound of the falling coins, the Church is literally silent. Through his use of symbolism, Joyce suggests that the Church is spiritually silent, as well.

William Butler Yeats, The Second Coming

Yeats believed that the Christian era that began with the birth of Christ would last for 2000 years, after which an anti-Christ would appear and an era of suffering and hardship would begin. "The Second Coming" describes the arrival of this anti-Christ.

One of the poem's main symbols is a falcon that spirals away from its master, the falconer. This broken connection suggests a loss of control and the concomitant social and political chaos, which Yeats saw as endemic in the early years of the twentieth century when this poem was written. "The best lack all conviction," he laments, "while the worst / Are full of passionate intensity" (lines 7–8). Echoing the Book of Revelation, the poem concludes with another religious symbol. Yeats describes an evil sphinx-like creature, which awakens in the desert and "Slouches toward Bethlehem to be born" (line 22). The Christian era is over, conquered by a satanic presence that will rule for the next 2000 years.

CHARACTER AS SYMBOL

A character in a literary work occasionally does double duty, as both a participant in the action and as a symbol that transcends action and suggests deeper meaning. Archetypal or

stereotypical characters, discussed in Chapter 5, are examples of one type of symbolic characters. Other examples are
discussed in this section.

John Cheever, The Swimmer

"The Swimmer" is the story of Neddy Merrill, a man who
realizes, one sunny Sunday while he is visiting neighbors,
that he could practically swim back to his own house via his
neighbors' swimming pools. He sets off to do just that.

At first, everything goes smoothly. His neighbors are
friendly and, in their way, cheer him on. But as he gets closer to his own home, ominous signs begin to appear. Neighbors begin to shun him; an ex-mistress verbally assaults him.
He has to make a harrowing run across a highway to continue his journey. He has to swim in the public pool where the
lifeguards disparage him. When he finally arrives home, he
discovers his house is deserted and decrepit, and his family
is gone. He has, moreover, visibly aged though the action occurs within a single afternoon. And summer has given way
to late autumn.

Ned Merrill is a symbol of a broken American dream, of an
optimism that is really self-deception, and of the innocence
of youth spoiled by the travails of aging. At the beginning of
the story he appears trim and athletic, eager to swim the
eight miles back home, and romantic enough to name his
imaginary river the Lucinda, after his wife. But as Ned gets
closer to his goal, readers begin to realize his journey is a
fantasy. He has suffered some kind of business reversal that
he has refused to accept. He has become something of a social outcast, now that he has lost the wealth by which his
friends measured him. Even his family has deserted him. The
American dream is superficial and transitory but so important that Ned refuses to believe his is over.

Eudora Welty, Livvie

"Livvie" is the story of a young black woman who marries
Solomon, a much older man who takes her off to live on a se-
cluded farm. She is only sixteen when the story begins. Some
years go by and Solomon grows old and finally confines himself to his bed, while Livvie remains young and vibrant. A
cosmetics saleswoman visits the farmhouse and tempts
Livvie with her lipstick. A handsome young farmworker
named Cash appears, and Livvie is attracted to him. They
visit Solomon who is furious to see the two of them together. Apparently, his system cannot handle the shock because
he actually dies while they are in his presence. Cash and

Livvie leave the room and embrace, drawn irresistibly to each other.

Livvie, as her name suggests, is a symbol of a young life yet to be "lived." Taken from her home as an adolescent girl, she has to spend her life thereafter basically as a nursemaid to an old man. Cash offers her life. His name is also symbolic, suggesting as it does the materiality of the outside world Livvie is just now beginning to encounter.

Nathaniel Hawthorne, Young Goodman Brown

Goodman Brown, the main character in Hawthorne's classic story, is both a character and a symbol. He is a young man, recently married, on his way to a Black Mass. He is ashamed of the evil thoughts that draw him toward the devil but stunned to meet so many people he knows from his village of Salem, who are also on their way to participate in the Mass. In fact, they are all looking forward to the initiation of the latest converts. Several times throughout the story, Brown hesitates, but the forces of darkness are too much for him. Eventually, he learns that he will not be the only new convert on this night, that a young woman will also be initiated into the ways of evil. When the woman turns out to be his wife, ironically named Faith, he knows he is lost. But just as Faith is about to commit herself to Satan, a puff of smoke clouds the forest and Goodman Brown finds himself back home in Salem. Readers are left to wonder if the experience was real or a dream. Whatever the case, Brown is a changed man from that time forward. He becomes a bitter man, an eternal pessimist, who can never find happiness.

Goodman Brown is a character in a story, but also a symbol of a certain psychological frame of mind. Brown is tempted by sin and ashamed of his weakness. To atone for his guilt he decides, subconsciously, that if he is tempted, everyone else must be as well. If everyone is tempted by sin, no one can be good. If no one is good, how is it possible to have faith, hope, and charity? Brown is the stereotypical pessimist who goes through life perpetually gloomy and embittered because he has to believe, as the devil tells him, that "evil is the nature of mankind."

The symbolism of Brown's character turns "Young Goodman Brown" into something of an **allegory.** An allegory is a story in which the characters and events extend beyond the confines of their story to represent an object lesson to readers. Characters' names often telegraph the nature of the lesson. In Bunyan's *The Pilgrim's Progress,* for example, the main character is Christian who is told by Evangelist to seek the

Celestial City. On his way, he encounters such people as Faithful, Hopeful, and Giant Despair. The object lesson in *The Pilgrim's Progress* is that personal salvation is available only through a commitment to Christ. Similarly, in "Young Goodman Brown" there is a character named Faith whom Goodman Brown doubts and ultimately turns away from. The object lesson in this story is that if you don't look for the good in people, you are likely to lose your faith in your own humanity.

Tone

Tone (sometimes called "voice") refers to the attitude or personality that a literary work projects. The tone can be serious and solemn, as it is in Milton's *Paradise Lost* (see Chapter 2), or lighthearted and amusing, as it is in Hardy's "The Ruined Maid" (see Chapter 4). Tone is the product of the subject of a literary work and the way in which the writer uses language—imagery, metaphor, diction—to describe the subject. In poetry, the rhythm and meter of the lines can also influence the tone. The subject of Elizabeth Barrett Browning's sonnet "How Do I Love Thee" (see Chapter 8) is the spiritual nature of her love for her husband, and Barrett Browning uses expansive imagery, religious metaphors, repetition, and slow-moving iambic lines to establish the poem's serene and confident tone. Between the two extremes of solemn and lighthearted are other common literary voices including those that project resignation, sorrow, irony, and triumph.

SORROW

When a writer deals with a sad subject, the tone of his or her poem or story will reflect that sorrow.

William Butler Yeats, When You Are Old

The subject of Yeats's poem "When You Are Old" is the death of love. The poet addresses a woman he loved, inviting her, when she is old and gray, to read his work and remember the love he had for her. It was a special, spiritual love; he was the one man to love the "pilgrim soul" (line 7) in her. She will be sad to realize that love has gone, and she will remember wistfully the promise of their youth.

The tone of "When You Are Old" perfectly complements its subject. The dominant image of an old woman falling asleep beside the fire and reading a book of the author's poems conveys an impression of loneliness and sorrow. The personification (see Chapter 9) of love fleeing over the mountain and hiding "amid a crowd of stars" (line 12) reinforces the sense of loss the woman must feel. The slow-moving iambic pentameter lines help establish the sense of the lethargy of old age. The imagery, metaphors, and rhythm combine to create the sad and wistful tone the poem so appropriately conveys.

John Keats, Bright Star

Keats was a young man, only 21, when he wrote this sonnet. He suffered from tuberculosis and knew he would not have a long life. He died, in fact, in 1821, soon after his twenty-third birthday. "Bright Star" reverberates with the sorrow the poet feels over what he knows will be a too brief life. He is especially sad that he will not live to consummate his feelings for a loved one. He envies the bright star, which is "steadfast" (line 1) and eternal, in contrast to what he knows will be his own premature mortality.

The sorrowful tone comes from the circumstances the poem describes: a young man in love, unable to fulfill that love because he does not have long to live. It comes as well from the image of the lone star lighting the sky and the ocean and the snow-covered earth below and from the way in which Keats contrasts the star's isolation with his own desire to avoid loneliness, to be, instead, "Pillowed upon [his] fair love's ripening breast" (line 11). And it comes from the pace of the rhythm of the lines, which is slow and deliberate, especially in the sonnet's final couplet.

Katherine Mansfield, Miss Brill

Mansfield's story begins amidst a pleasant tone created by the circumstances of an older woman enjoying a day in the park and relishing the music provided by the local band. The tone changes after a young couple joins Miss Brill on the park bench and insensitively make fun of her appearance, especially of the fox stole she wears. Poor Miss Brill returns to her lonely apartment, her happiness shattered by the comments of the young people. The comments were disrespectful and insolent, but they make Miss Brill realize that she appears as a figure of fun to some people and this is enough to generate the tears of sorrow with which the story ends and which intensifies the story's sorrowful voice.

RESIGNATION

The tone of some literary works will help convey the sense that, even if life is not ideal, it is necessary to accept the way things are. In other words, a writer will use a certain voice to help convey a sense that he or she is resigned to the reality of a certain situation.

Nikki Giovanni, Woman

The woman at the center of Giovanni's poem does all she can to make her partner into the man she wants him to be. She wants commitment, support, friendship, and compassion. But she never seems to get from him what she wants. So she "decided to become / a woman" (lines 18–19). She resigns herself to the realization that he will never be the man she hoped he would be. The implication is that by becoming a woman, in the true sense of the word, she will fulfill all of the needs and desires she had previously counted on a man to fulfill for her.

William Shakespeare, When My Love Swears that She Is Made of Truth

The speaker of Shakespeare's Sonnet 138 expresses concern about his declining years and the consequent infidelity of his girlfriend. He knows she lies to him but he ostensibly believes her lies. She, in turn, flatters his youthful appearance when they both know he is well past his prime. They have an unspoken agreement: He will overlook her infidelity, and she will overlook the loss of his youth and vitality. In this way, they maintain their sexual relationship—"lie" with each other—even while they tell lies to each other.

> Therefore I lie with her and she with me,
> And in our faults by lies we flattered be.
> (lines 13–14)

The relationship obviously is far from ideal, but it works because they both play the game.

The tone of this sonnet is one of resignation and acceptance. The speaker could be sad about his relationship with his friend, but he is not. The pun on the word "lie" with which the sonnet concludes undercuts any sorrow he might have otherwise expressed. He is shrugging his shoulders and saying his relationship is far from perfect but better than having no relationship at all. The tone of the poem conveys this rather carefree and accepting, if not contented, attitude.

IRONY

The tone of a work of literature is ironic when events do not unfold as they should, usually because a character refuses or is unable to recognize deception in another character or a deficiency in him- or herself.

Dorothy Parker, One Perfect Rose

The speaker in Parker's poem "One Perfect Rose" describes the perfect rose "with scented dew still wet" her admirer sends her. Along with the rose is a tender and endearing proclamation of love. The irony is that a perfect rose is not what she wants, as the poem's final stanza makes clear:

> Why is it no one ever sent me yet
> One perfect limousine, do you suppose?
> Ah no, it's always just my luck to get
> One perfect rose.
> (lines 9–12)

The tone of this poem actually changes from beginning to end. It begins as a love poem with roses and heartfelt sentiment, and the diction—"tenderly," "deep-hearted," "pure," "love"—conveys a decidedly romantic tone. In the last stanza the tone changes with the phrase "one perfect limousine" and becomes humorous and ironic. By the end of the poem, the one perfect rose has become more a source of exasperation rather than a symbol of romance. Ironically, this woman prefers expensive presents over romantic ones.

Lorrie Moore, How to Become a Writer

Moore's story is a good example of not only ironic content but also of an ironic writing style. It is about the struggle of a young woman, a college freshman, to become a writer. Her challenges come mainly in the form of friends and teachers who critique her work ruthlessly, undercut her enthusiasm, and generally make her question her talent. These friends and teachers are described ironically and the narrator's incisive descriptions of them make "How to Become a Writer" a very funny story.

Moore's style adds to the ironic tone. Her sentences are uniformly short and witty. They read like the words of a stand-up comic delivering punch lines. The story is written in the present tense, creating a sense of events that have not already occurred but that are occurring while we are reading the story.

Wilfred Owen, Dulce et Decorum Est

A writer can use irony to add either humor or sarcasm to his or her work. In "Dulce et Decorum Est," Owen uses the latter. Set on the First World War battlefield, the poem describes a gruesome and deadly gas attack. The narrator watches young men struggle to put on gas masks and observes the agony of those soldiers who fail to get their masks on in time.

He ends the poem expressing grave doubts about the extent to which anyone who could see what he sees could agree with Horace's dictum that it is a sweet and glorious thing (dulce et decorum est) to die for one's country. Horace's ostensibly stirring Latin epigraph delivered in the context of young men being poisoned to death provides the poem with its intensely ironic ending.

TRIUMPH

Literature is often inspirational. It tells of the power of faith, of courage overcoming seemingly insurmountable obstacles, of the strength of the human spirit. In such poems and stories, a triumphant voice is usually present.

G. K. Chesterton, The Donkey

G. K. Chesterton's poem is told from the point of view of the donkey who bemoans his homely physical appearance: "The devils walking parody / On all four-footed things" (lines 7–8). Other living things, the donkey continues, mock his discordant bray and foolish ears. But "I also had my hour," the donkey continues: "On Palm Sunday, it was upon my back that Christ rode into Jerusalem."

The tone of "The Donkey" changes between the third and last stanza. In the first three stanzas the tone of the poem is rather bitter, as the donkey describes the torment he has endured. The diction—"monstrous," "sickening," "tattered," "scourge"—establishes this bitter tone. Yet in the final stanza, the tone turns triumphant with the powerful image of the donkey bearing Christ into Jerusalem, while the people strew the way with palm branches and leaves. The tone helps to establish the theme of the poem: that physical beauty is irrelevant to the value of our actions.

Stephen Dunn, Tenderness

The narrator of Dunn's poem describes his relationship with an older woman whose violent husband is in prison. She craves tenderness and he, being only twenty-three, is

more interested simply in sex. But their relationship blossoms, and the narrator discovers the ecstasy of genuinely
caring for someone else. The tone of the poem is solemn until
the narrator discovers the emotional reward of tenderness,
at which point the tone changes, and the poem ends on a triumphant note. The relationship has given the narrator "new
hands and new sorrow" (line 43). He has become "a man
changed, unheroic, floating" (line 45).

The Author's Life and Times

If an author goes to jail, is elected to public office, observes or participates in a crucial historical event, or survives a personal tragedy, chances are he or she will write about it. An author's life and times inevitably influence his or her work. In this chapter, we will examine specific examples of how personal experience and historical circumstance have shaped a writer's work.

PERSONAL EXPERIENCE

Authors will often base a poem or a story on a significant personal experience. They usually change real names to fictitious ones, and they might alter the timeline or some other aspect of the original experience to create the effect they want. Many literary works are based upon a true story.

Richard Lovelace, To Althea, From Prison

"To Althea, From Prison" is a well-known poem, the appreciation of which is enhanced by some knowledge of the author's life. "To Althea, From Prison" was, in fact, written in a London jail where its author, Richard Lovelace, was incarcerated for presenting a pro-royalist petition to Parliament. It was April 1642. Parliament was fighting to increase its powers at the expense of the King's, and politicians were in no mood to receive, from a brazen twenty-four-year-old courtier from Kent, a petition in support of the policies of Charles I.

"To Althea, From Prison" is based on the paradox that the poet, though physically confined, is emotionally free because his love for Althea and his loyalty to his King transcend physical confinement. Lovelace expresses this sentiment in the poem's famous last stanza:

Stone walls do not a prison make,
    Nor iron bars a cage;
Minds innocent and quiet take
    That for an hermitage.
If I have freedom in my love,
    And in my soul am free,
Angels alone that soar above,
    Enjoy such liberty.

                          (1649)

The identity of Althea, if she is a real person, is not known. Young poets in the time of Charles I admired and paid poetic tribute to many women, some real, some ideal. Lovelace had Althea, Amaratha, Aramantha, and, especially, Lucasta whose relationship to Lovelace is discussed in more detail in the next section of this chapter.

William Butler Yeats, Among School Children

"Among School Children" also grew out of personal experience. In 1922, Yeats was appointed a senator of the newly created Irish Free State, and his public duties included an occasional visit to a school. On the visit that occasioned this poem, he tours a school, surrounded by schoolgirls whose youth and innocence make him think about the course of his own life. He remembers, as he did in so many of his poems, his unrequited love for the beautiful actress and Irish revolutionary Maud Gonne. Now, at the age of sixty, he wonders if his own mother would think of his life as

A compensation for the pang of his birth,
Or the uncertainty of his setting forth.
(lines 39–40)

He speculates on the purpose of life, on the conditions under which "Labour is blossoming or dancing" (line 56), in other words, the conditions under which life is full and meaningful. He considers religion, philosophy, and parenthood as possible sources for life's meaning and relevance. But, he asks, "How can we know the dancer from the dance?" (line 63). In other words, how can we separate abstract concepts such as religion and philosophy from human experience, which gives the abstract concepts real expression? He concludes that nothing alone can give life meaning but that all of life's elements—the life of the mind and the life of the spirit—dancing together give us the purpose and harmony we need to live productively.

John Milton, Methought I Saw My Late Espoused Saint

"Methought I Saw My Late Espoused Saint" is another example of a poem based on personal experience. Milton's eyesight was always weak and, by 1651, at the age of 43, he was completely blind. In 1656, four years after his first wife died in childbirth, he married Katherine Woodcock. In 1658, she, too, died in childbirth. These two tragic events, his blindness and the death of his second wife, influenced the composition of his sonnet, "Methought I Saw My Late Espoused Saint."

In the poem, he describes a dream he had during which his late wife Katherine comes to him "vested all in white, pure as her mind" (line 9). His love and desire for her is overwhelming, but as he reaches out to return her embrace, she flees, he wakes up and confronts again the reality that he can never see her or anyone else again:

> But O, as to embrace me she inclined,
> I waked, she fled, and day brought back my night.
> (lines 13–14)

Milton married a third time in 1663 and, despite his blindness, wrote the great epic poem in our language *Paradise Lost* (see Chapter 2) and a sequel *Paradise Regained* before his death in 1674.

VALUES AND IDEALS

In addition to those life experiences discussed above, a writer might hold dear certain values and ideals and make his or her commitment to those ideals the subject of a poem or story.

Richard Lovelace, To Lucasta, Going to the Wars

In the previous section, you learned that Lovelace based some of his work on personal experience. He also, in his poetry, blended these personal experiences with his values and ideals.

The most famous of these, "To Lucasta, Going to the Wars," was written after Lovelace was released from prison. Upon his release, Lovelace resumed his career as an army officer. Before he was imprisoned, he had served King Charles I in two campaigns against Scotland. Now, in 1643, he became something of a soldier of fortune, and served with the French against the Spaniards in Holland. He probably wrote "To Lucasta, Going to the Wars" before he left England on one such campaign.

Lucasta (which means "chaste light") was probably Lucy Sacheverell to whom Lovelace might have been engaged and who he might have even married. Lovelace's friend and fellow poet, Sir John Suckling, mentions the marriage of his friend "Dick" in one of his poems. One story, also unauthenticated, has it that Lovelace was engaged to Lucy, but that she married someone else when she learned Lovelace had been killed in battle. In fact, Lovelace was alive, although he was wounded at Dunkirk, in October 1646.

In the poem, he apologizes to Lucasta for leaving her, justifying his behavior in the famous last stanza wherein he asserts that, before he can truly love her, he must acquire the self-respect that comes from his individual pursuit of honor:

> Yet this inconstancy is such
> > As you too shall adore;
> I could not love thee, dear, so much,
> > Loved I not honour more.

> (1649)

Honor was a high ideal among the Cavalier poets. They were a group of aristocratic young men loyal to the King, from whom they hoped to win patronage and an important and lucrative position in the government. They prided themselves on their well-roundedness: They were soldiers eager to distinguish themselves in battle and poets eager to heap praise on the many women who attracted their roving eyes. Lovelace, Sir John Suckling, Robert Herrick, and Edmund Waller are among the most famous of the Cavalier poets.

After the Dutch wars ended, Lovelace returned to England. In 1648, a series of rebellions occurred in support of Charles I, and Lovelace came under suspicion once again. His brothers, Francis and Dudley, were ardent Royalists, and Richard might have been the victim of guilt by association. At any rate, he was imprisoned again.

He was released April 10, 1649, but was apparently now a broken man. He disappeared from public view; little is known about the last part of his life. The date of his death is uncertain but probably occurred in 1657. His brother Francis edited his collection of posthumous poems, published in 1659.

OBSERVED EXPERIENCE

A writer might write about an event that he or she observed with great interest, even if that writer did not participate directly in the event.

Alexander Pope, The Rape of the Lock

In the summer of 1711, a group of affluent young men and women partied together, probably at the impressive north London home of one of the young people. At this party, Robert, Lord Petre, was so dazzled by two ringlets hanging from the back of the neck of Arabella Fermor that he took a pair of scissors and, when Arabella's back was turned, he cut off one of the locks.

Arabella was outraged and offended as were her parents when they learned of the incident. Both families, the Fermors and the Petres, were members of the close-knit Roman Catholic community, but their friendship became threatened because of what Lord Petre did. Another member of this community, its unofficial leader, was John Caryll who hated to see enmity within a community who had to stick together because they were always under the threat of religious persecution.

Alexander Pope was not at the party, but he was a member of this Roman Catholic extended family. Caryll knew the young poet (Pope was 23 at this time), and it was Caryll who suggested Pope write about the incident in such a way that the two families would realize the incident, while unfortunate, was too trivial to threaten an important friendship. Pope agreed and wrote the great mock epic poem in the English language.

An epic poem (see Chapter 2) is a long narrative that describes the heroic exploits of extraordinary people: brave soldiers, princesses, kings, and queens. Gods and goddesses are brought to life in epic poetry and intervene in the lives of the mortals and often determine the direction of the plot. A mock epic poem, then, is a narrative that satirizes people who magnify their ordinary lives and who think their actions are far more important and consequential than they really are.

Both Belinda, the Arabella character in *The Rape of the Lock,* and the Baron, the Lord Petre character, are egomaniacs who have exaggerated notions about the significance of their place and presence in the world. The Baron acts as if he has won great honor and glory on the battlefield after he cuts off Arabella's lock of hair. Arabella acts as if she has been sexually violated. A mock-epic battle between the men at the party and the women ensues after the rape of the lock. Pope's description of the battle, with both sides aided and abetted by supernatural sprites and fairies, is one of the outstanding examples of farce in the language. The battle ends when the lock of hair, the cause of all the discord, cannot be found. It has ascended into the heavens and become a constellation, an eternal tribute to Belinda's beauty.

Did the poem succeed in ending the hostility between the two families? Pope himself claimed that it did. Arabella apparently had some reservations about the propriety of the poem but abandoned them when Pope dedicated to her the expanded version he wrote in 1714. One of the characters, Sir George Browne who is Sir Plume in the poem, was furious about being portrayed as a blundering fool and actually threatened to beat Pope up. No doubt he was dissuaded by others who warned him that challenging a four-and-a-half-foot-tall deformed poet to a fight would do nothing for his reputation.

Pope would go on, despite his poor health, to compose a great body of satiric and philosophic poetry. He died in 1744.

HISTORICAL CIRCUMSTANCE

Writers are influenced by the times in which they live and work. If a historically significant event takes place during an author's life, that event and the author's "take" on that event might become the subject of a poem, a story, or a play.

John Milton, On the Late Massacre at Piedmont

Milton was a supporter of Oliver Cromwell who led the Puritan Revolt that ousted King Charles I from power in 1649. Cromwell rewarded Milton with a cabinet post, Secretary for Foreign Tongues. One of Milton's duties was to write letters to foreign officials articulating Britain's position on certain world events.

On April 24, 1655, a religious sect known as the Waldenses, who lived in the Piedmont Valley of northern Italy, were attacked and slaughtered by Italian troops, acting on behalf of a government who felt that the Waldenses' Protestant beliefs were a threat to Roman Catholicism, even though the Waldenses had lived peacefully in Piedmont for some years. Milton was furious over the attack and made official protests in his capacity as Cromwell's cabinet minister. He also wrote a sonnet ("On the Late Massacre in Piedmont") to protest the Italian government's appalling action.

The sonnet is in the form of a plea to God to avenge the death of the Waldenses. He sees them as martyrs to the Protestant faith. Milton's own anti-Catholicism comes out in his criticism of Catholic worship of graven images (the "stocks and stones" of line 4) and his suspicion that the Pope, "The triple tyrant" (line 12; "triple" is an allusion to the Pope's three-crowned hat), was complicit in the attack. He ends the sonnet expressing the hope that from the blood and ashes of the martyrs one hundred times as many Protestants will spring to fight Catholic persecution.

An Introduction to Methods of Literary Analysis

English professors and literary critics have designed a number of methods of analyzing literary texts to deepen their own understanding of poetry, fiction, and drama and to share their understanding with students and other readers. They designed these analytical methods to help readers understand literature, to illustrate how the language of a literary text enhances meaning, to examine the role of literature within society, and to study the complex relationships among authors, texts, and readers. It is important for you, as a student of literature, to know something about these analytical methods. This knowledge will help you understand and appreciate the literature you are studying and help you express that knowledge in your essays and in-class discussions. Ten of the common methods of literary analysis are discussed in this chapter:

- Formalism
- Structuralism
- Psychoanalytic criticism
- Archetypal criticism
- Reader-response criticism
- Marxist criticism
- Feminist criticism
- Gay/Lesbian criticism
- Deconstruction
- New Historicism

FORMALISM

Formalism (also called New Criticism) emerged as a method of literary analysis in the 1920s, at a time when literature was becoming an important academic discipline. There arose a need at this time for rigorous methods of analysis to legitimize the place of literary studies within the academy and to help students and other readers understand increasingly complex poems, stories, and plays. New Criticism is no longer new, but it remains an influential school of literary criticism.

Formalists focus their attention on the text itself, virtually ignoring extratextual influences such as the author's life and times and the reader's personal beliefs and experiences. A literary work should have a central unifying theme and all other elements of the work should contribute to that theme, creating what New Critics refer to as "organic unity." They urge readers to examine a literary work closely and intensely, focusing on and analyzing the elements of literature such as plot, character, point of view, metaphor, rhythm, imagery, and symbolism. Formalists argue that a poem, a story, or a play is a self-contained work of art, comprehensible when readers examine a work intensely and understand how the parts fit together to form a unified whole. They believe that the quality of a literary work can be evaluated, based on the extent to which the language—the imagery, metaphors, symbols—intensifies and augments the theme.

According to Formalists, a literary work reflects reality; a story, for example, mirrors reality and gives readers insight into genuine human experience.

John Keats, La Belle Dame Sans Merci: A Ballad

"La Belle Dame Sans Merci" is a narrative poem about a knight who is sick and depressed because he has been deceived by a woman. This is no ordinary woman, however. It is la belle dame sans merci, that is, the beautiful woman without mercy or pity. She is "a fairy's child" (line 14) who seduces the knight and then abandons him. He gives her gifts; she sings to him and feeds him exotic dishes. She takes him to her grotto where they become lovers. He sleeps and dreams of "death pale" (line 38) kings, princes, and soldiers who warn the knight about la belle dame's enchantment over him. In the morning he finds himself abandoned and alone, feeling unwell, beside a cold and desolate lake.

The beautiful woman without mercy is a metaphor for the poet's muse. A muse is a source of inspiration for artistic creation. A poet loves and romances his muse, follows her, pledges his allegiance to her. She, in turn, toys with him. At times, she, too, adores him and serves him as he wants to be served, by stimulating the poet's artistic abilities. But, just as quickly, she will abandon him, leaving him lonely and devoid of the poetic inspiration he needs to be creative. The knight-at-arms' muse sings to him, seduces him, but finally abandons him. "No birds sing" (last line), and, for now, at least, no poets write.

"La Belle Dame Sans Merci" is a ballad and contains the traditional ballad characteristics. It tells a story; it is written in quatrains, twelve in all; it has the typical *abcb* ballad rhyme scheme and the iambic tetrameter rhythm and meter. It contains an element of the supernatural: a beautiful woman with mysterious powers—an enchantress. It is unique in that the last line of each quatrain contains two or three beats, not the four of the other tetrameter lines. Keats uses spondees liberally in the last lines of each stanza: "And no birds sing" (line 4); "On the cold hill's side" (lines 36 and 44). The emphasis and the truncation of these lines brilliantly highlight the sense of loss the knight feels after his muse has abandoned him.

STRUCTURALISM

Structuralist critics believe that the human psyche is a well-organized construct and that the literary works humans produce reflect this internal order. Structuralists, then, seek meaning by examining and analyzing the structure of a literary work. One major way in which we structure reality is through a bipolar perception: light and dark, day and night, hero and villain, man and woman, realist and romantic. Consequently, a major method structuralists use to interpret a text is to examine how the tension between opposites contributes to meaning.

Structuralists share some of the views of New Critics, believing, for example, in close and detailed readings. Unlike New Critics, however, Structuralists do not believe that literature is referential, that is, that literature reflects reality. They believe a literary work creates its own reality and is meaningful only within that limited space. Whether or not a literary work says something important about life in general is not important to Structuralists.

Structuralism is more a scientific than a humanistic approach to literary analysis, influenced as it is by the structural linguistics of Ferdinand de Saussure. Every literary work is a separate "system." Structuralists speak about the "grammar" of literary work, the way plot elements combine to create a textual structure. The reader/critic's task is to determine how the parts within the system, the words, relate to and ricochet off each other to create meaning.

Structuralists avoid value judgments. New Critics judge the quality of a work based on the extent to which the parts coalesce into a meaningful whole. Structuralists are concerned less with the integrity and more with the nature of the structure itself.

Stephen Crane, The Blue Hotel

To a point, the structure of Crane's story resembles the structure of a paperback Western novel. Three strangers arrive at the Blue Hotel in the small town of Fort Romper, Nebraska. They play poker with the proprietor's son. One of the strangers, the Swede, has a romantic notion of the reputation of the Wild West and fears for his own safety. He considers leaving but gets drunk and continues the poker game. He accuses the proprietor's son, Johnny, of cheating. They fight and the bigger Swede wins. Flushed with his success, he swings into a saloon and insists the patrons drink with him. They refuse. Annoyed, he tries to force the local gambler into drinking with him. They scuffle; the gambler draws a knife and kills the Swede. He is sentenced to three years in prison.

A traditional Western might end here, but Crane adds a final chapter, that introduces the kind of moral dilemma not usually found in the typical Western. Chapter IX occurs months after the Swede's death. The two strangers discuss the death and the sentence of the gambler. Then one of the strangers, the Easterner, tells the other, the cowboy, that Johnny was in fact cheating. He could have prevented the tragedy, but he chose not to speak up. Scully, the owner, and the cowboy were blind to what was happening. Only the gambler, a minor player in the story, pays the price for a crime in which four other men were complicit. Crane's story transcends the Western genre to become a comment on community versus individual responsibility. Had the community acted responsibly, the Swede's death would have been prevented and the gambler's family would not have been deprived of its provider. Crane parodies the rugged individualism so valued in American society, implying instead that there is a collective moral obligation to act.

Structurally, then, Crane's story is pulp fiction enclosed within a larger form of a work of serious, naturalistic fiction. The first eight chapters carry the plot, which begins with the arrival of the Swede and ends with his death. The ninth chapter at once summarizes the action and introduces the moral dilemma that becomes the story's frame:

I: Three new guests come to the Blue Hotel.
II: They play cards with the proprietor's son; the Swede acts strangely, fearing he will be murdered.

  III: The proprietor, Scully, tries to talk the Swede into stay-
        ing.
  IV: They get drunk together and the Swede, to the amaze-
        ment of the others, apparently decides to stay.
   V: The Swede accuses Johnny of cheating; Johnny chal-
        lenges him to a fight.
  VI: The fight occurs; the Swede wins.
 VII: The Swede leaves the Blue Hotel.
VIII: He goes to a bar; the gambler refuses to drink with him;
        he manhandles the gambler, who knifes him to death.
  IX: The cowboy and the Easterner discuss the gambler's
        light sentence; the Easterner confirms Johnny was
        cheating.

The Swede is the main character is the story, yet curi-
ously, he is as much antagonist as protagonist. He is the classic bully whose courage really only kicks in when he has had
too much to drink. He gloats about his victory over Johnny
who is not much more than a boy. He is aggressive towards
the gambler who overreacts when he kills the Swede but
whose light sentence is no doubt the result of a reasonable
self-defense argument.

The Easterner uses a curious metaphor to describe the
gambler and his role in the story. He is not a noun, the Easterner says, merely an adverb. The metaphor encourages the
reader to view the structure of the story as a simple sentence. The community, consisting of Johnny, Scully, the Easterner, the cowboy, and the bartender, is the subject. The
gambler is a member of the community, as well, but something of an outsider by virtue of his profession and his curious mix of dispassionate aloofness and solid citizenship.
"Murder" is the verb. "The Swede" is the object. Reduced to
a sentence the story's structure is: "The community dispassionately murders the Swede."

PSYCHOANALYTIC CRITICISM

Psychoanalytic critics apply the psychological theories of Sig-
mund Freud (1856–1939) to the author of a work of literature
and to the characters who live within a work of literature in
order to explain the meaning of the text to its readers. Freud
believed that a work of literature is a product of its author's
subconscious needs and desires and that characters in literature act and react according to their subconscious needs
and desires. The critic's task is to make the text meaningful
by psychoanalyzing the author and the characters the author has created. The critic studies the author's childhood

and life experiences to determine what seminal events might have influenced the author's creative process. The psychoanalytic critic also studies the characters' lives and the nature of their interactions with others.

Henry James, The Turn of the Screw

James's story is about an English country house haunted by the ghosts of a valet and a governess who once worked at the house but who have since died, under somewhat mysterious circumstances. A new governess, who is the story's narrator, comes to take charge of the education of the two children. It is she who sees the ghosts and most of the story recounts her attempts to keep the children immune from the evil the ghosts manifest. She is ultimately unsuccessful.

Psychoanalytic critics read the narrator/governess as a neurotic, sexually repressed young woman. She is the twenty-year-old daughter of a country parson and she is not at all experienced in the ways of the world. The two children in her charge are beautiful and she is attracted to them, to the boy, Miles, especially, in inappropriate ways. She is also attracted to the children's uncle, who is their guardian, although he does not live with them. This attraction produces guilt, which is repressed but which manifests itself in her hallucinations. She imagines she sees the ghosts of the valet and of her predecessor; the two were lovers before the valet died and the former governess left the employ of the children's uncle. The new governess sees the valet upon the tower, a Freudian phallic symbol, and the former governess across the lake, a Freudian symbol of female sexuality. The little girl, Flora, makes a toy boat by pushing a stick into a flat piece of wood, suggesting, subconsciously of course, sexual intercourse, which is at once abhorrent and intriguing to the narrator.

The narrator's neurosis has a profound effect upon the children, since she is their primary caregiver. They don't really see the ghosts themselves, the psychoanalytic critics argue, but they become victims of their governess's bizarre behavior that results from her emotional turmoil. Flora leaves the home, ill; and Miles dies as much from fright as from any physical illness.

Edgar Allan Poe, The Cask of Amontillado

Montresor, the narrator of Poe's story, suffers from envy and an inferiority complex, which causes him to resent the success of others and seek their destruction. He also projects onto others the character flaws he himself possesses.

Projection, according to Freud, is a common human idiosyncrasy whereby we invest others with a flaw we ourselves possess.

Montresor's victim is Fortunato whom Montresor accuses of a "thousand injuries" though the nature of those injuries is never specified, and Fortunato is himself clearly oblivious to any of them, because he willingly accompanies Montresor to his home. Fortunato's real crime is that he is "rich, respected, admired, and beloved," as Montresor is not. He is, as well, a member of the Masonic Order, as Montresor is not. In his twisted way, Montresor imagines that he has been denied wealth, respect, and friendship because Fortunato possesses them, and so he resolves to murder Fortunato. He lures him into his cellars on the pretext of verifying the quality of a cask of amontillado wine Montresor has purchased. When they are in the furthest reaches of the cellars, Montresor shackles Fortunato to the cave and proceeds to seal him in behind a brick wall.

Montresor is a psychopath. He has convinced himself that Fortunato has wronged him grievously and believes he is therefore justified in taking Fortunato's life.

ARCHETYPAL CRITICISM

Archetypal critics apply the theories of the Swiss psychoanalyst Carl Jung (1875–1961) to the study of literature. Jungian critics believe that every human psyche imbeds certain shared experiences, giving all of us a universal or collective unconscious. Writers therefore inevitably tell the same archetypal stories over and over again and populate those stories with the same archetypal characters. Readers will recognize those stories as universal, as shared products of a collective unconscious, and that recognition will mediate the way in which they interpret and understand literary works. The quest for self-knowledge and spiritual enlightenment, the rescue, and the story of creation are examples of archetypal plots. The hero, the villain, the damsel in distress, the wise old man, the braggart, the mysterious stranger, the seducer, the lazy slob, and the hypocrite are examples of archetypal characters who recur in literary works because we recognize them. Because they recur, we can better understand the literary works they inhabit.

Archetypal criticism is most useful as a way of linking texts together. The method urges the reader to connect the text he or she is studying with other texts with similar plots and characters, to better understand individual works and the literary imagination in general.

William Faulkner, Barn Burning

"Barn Burning" is the archetypal story of the son rebelling against a father whose values and ideals the son finds intolerable. It is a story that goes back at least as far as the Bible and that surfaces throughout the literature of all countries. Shakespeare, Dickens, Turgenev, Henry James, Hemingway, and James Joyce are among the many fiction writers who have told similar stories.

The father is Abner Snopes and the son, Sarty. Abner is a poor sharecropper who vents his anger and frustration over his poverty by violating the personal property of those he believes have wronged him. Usually, he seeks the revenge that he imagines is due to him by burning down the barns of those who have offended him.

Sarty is torn between his blood loyalty to his father and his knowledge that what his father is doing is wrong. When Abner decides to burn the barn of Major de Spain, Sarty decides to act. His father, suspicious of the boy's loyalty, orders his wife and daughters to hold Sarty, but he escapes and warns de Spain who chases off the arsonists.

Abner resembles another archetypal character, one who appears and reappears in various guises throughout the literature of every culture: Satan. Abner's element is fire, not the fire of creation but the fire of destruction, the fire of hell. He resembles the devil, dressed as he is in his stiff black suit. His limp, the remnant of a Civil War gunshot wound, suggests the devil's cloven hoof. His behavior, certainly, is satanic. He lives, it seems, to harm those who, he believes, have sinned against him, and he inflicts that harm with a satanic dispassion.

There are archetypal stories of sons who admire their fathers and who want to emulate them; there are archetypal stories of sons who see in their fathers the very man they do not want to become. "Barn Burning" is, of course, an example of the latter. Sarty is still too young to articulate the contempt he has for his father, too young and naïve to understand the nature of evil. But his actions indicate his resolve to rebel against the contempt for the rights of others and the satanic hostility his father personifies.

READER-RESPONSE CRITICISM

Reader-response critics are not concerned so much with explicating a literary text as they are with insisting upon the reader's right to interpret a text in a way that makes sense to that reader. Reader-response theory has its roots in **phenomenology,** a philosophy that asserts that human consciousness is unique to each individual, and that, therefore, everyone perceives reality differently. Different readers have different values, ideals, political beliefs, genders, ethnic origins, ages, and life experiences. All of these color the way we read.

Reader-response critics believe that the meaning of a literary text lies primarily within the head of the reader, and that the text is merely the medium the reader manipulates to make his or her world meaningful. Readers do not so much "decode" as "encode" a literary text. Reading is a creative process; a reader rewrites the text. Every decoding, reader-responders insist, is another encoding. They stress response rather than interpretation.

Reader-response theorists do not, however, abrogate the reader's responsibility to the text and the author. Theirs is not an "anything goes" philosophy in that they urge readers to bring knowledge to texts and to learn what needs to be learned to understand and appreciate literature. The concept of the informed and the competent reader is important to reader-response theorists.

There are a number of special-interest groups within the reader-response critical field. Some readers believe strongly in a political or social philosophy, so strongly that these beliefs define their lives, and, hence, determine the way they read. Marxist and feminist critics, for example, filter their analysis of literary texts through the lens of their Marxism and feminism. Gay/lesbian critics, similarly, read literature in the context of their own lifestyle because it determines their identity so strongly.

Emily Dickinson, I Like to See It Lap the Miles

In this poem, Dickinson describes an object or a force of nature, perhaps, traveling swiftly across the countryside. The object traverses hills and valleys, makes a loud noise, and finally comes to rest. Some readers believe the poet is describing a horse because the "it" that is lapping the miles "neighs" (line 14), runs laps (line 1), and returns "to its own stable door" (line 17).

Other readers believe the poet is describing a river. "It" "lick[s] the Valleys Up" (line 2) and "stop[s] to feed itself at tanks" (line 2), which could be a reference to lakes. It flows down and between mountains and makes a noise like the noise described in the poem, especially if the river becomes a waterfall at any point in its journey. And, at the end of its journey, a river stops "docile and omnipotent / At its own stable door" (lines 16–17), which could be a reference to the ocean.

Other readers believe the poet is describing a train. The object Dickinson describes moves like a train, in that it "lick[s] the Valleys Up" (line 2), travels through the countryside, pares a Quarry (line 8), and "chase[s] itself down Hill" (line 13). It sounds like a train as well, "Complaining all the while / In horrid-hooting stanza" (lines 12–13) and "neigh[ing] like Boanerges" (line 14).

Biographical evidence does suggest that Dickinson did have a train in mind when, in about 1862, she wrote the poem. She describes in a letter to her brother how she was present when the rail line was officially opened in Amherst, and one of the first trains seen in the area left its station. In the first collection of her poetry, published in 1891, five years after her death, the poem is called "The Railway Train," though the editors, not Dickinson herself, titled it.

A train, then, is the most likely referent for the pronoun "it," but Dickinson's poem is brilliantly ambiguous, to the extent that it can support other interpretations as well.

MARXIST CRITICISM

Karl Marx (1818–1883) was a German political philosopher who believed that the capitalist system created an imbalance of power in society, which would lead to an iniquitous and inequitable class system. The iniquity of this system would lead to revolution, as the lower classes, unwilling to be economically enslaved, would rise up and overthrow the upper classes.

Marxist critics read literature in the context of the class struggle. More specifically, they use literature to reveal the exploitative and corrupt nature of the capitalist system, its superficial worship of material prosperity, and its consequent inequitable distribution of economic resources and social power.

Marxist critics focus on how the social class to which a writer belongs influences his or her artistic expression and on how social class and the desire for upward social mobility influences the motives and interpersonal relationships of literary characters. Marxist critics often begin by focusing on a work of literature, then eventually move away from that work to discuss the effect of social class in general.

Marxist critics are usually up-front about their motives. Their aim is not only to interpret a literary work but also to use literary criticism as a springboard to social revolution.

Tillie Olsen, I Stand Here Ironing

"I Stand Here Ironing" is a relentlessly sad story about a poor single mother raising five children. The story focuses on her first-born, Emily, who is a baby at the beginning of the story and a nineteen-year-old at the end, the same age her mother was when Emily was born. The mother is the story's narrator. The story starts in the Depression 1930s, progresses through the war years, and ends in the 1950s.

The narrator is poor when Emily is born and poorer still after her husband deserts her. There are no social programs, no welfare, no subsidized day care to alleviate poverty. Emily must go to live with her father's family while her mother struggles to survive through poorly paid jobs without any benefits. A sickly child, Emily is sent to a convalescent home, where she is desperately unhappy, for part of her childhood. Brothers and sisters arrive, taking more of her mother's attention away from her. She discovers a talent as a stand-up comedian, but she has no network to help her nurture the talent. As a nineteen-year-old in postwar America, she worries about the atom bomb destroying the world. Her mother, the narrator, sums up her life: "She is a child of her age, of depression, of war, of fear."

"I Stand Here Ironing" is a bitter indictment against the American capitalist system. The story illustrates the extent to which an economic system based upon an imbalance of power can destroy the individual spirit. The narrator is a woman broken by a system that exploits her labor for wages that can barely support one person let alone a growing family. The government, accomplices in an economic system that assures a gap between the rich and the poor, offers no social programs to alleviate the despair of the poor. Indeed, the government is doubly culpable, promoting as it does a system that led to the Great Depression and the Second World War, two events that figure prominently in the plot of the story and that magnify the plight of the narrator and her family. Olsen's story rings with a cry for the kind of revolution that will engender policy changes that will, in turn, force the redistribution of wealth in such a way that the rich are forced to share their wealth for the benefit of society as a whole.

Allen Ginsberg, A Supermarket in California

In "A Supermarket in California," Allen Ginsberg describes an experience he had shopping, or rather shoplifting, in a typical American supermarket. He finds himself inside this monument to American consumerism and feels like an alien among middle-class families doing their grocery shopping, loading their cars, and returning to their suburban houses.

A conservative reader would likely be critical of the poem's narrator, condemn his shoplifting, his admiration for gay poet Walt Whitman, and the indolent attitude that has led to his rootless existence. By rejecting mainstream society, the narrator lies down in the bed of loneliness he has made for himself.

A Marxist reader would likely view the narrator as something of a hero, a soldier in the war against corporate consumerism, who gets even with the capitalists by stealing from them. His alienation and loneliness is not sad or pathetic but symptomatic of a deliberate choice he has made, his protest against a social order he rejects. His rootless existence is a badge of honor, a mark of his refusal to join the middle class in the relentless quest for more, which can only mean that others will get less.

"A Supermarket in California" is a good example of a poem, the meaning of which changes diametrically, according the political philosophy of its readers.

FEMINIST CRITICISM

The aim of feminist critics is to promote women writers, especially those who have been overshadowed in the past by their male counterparts. They also use literary criticism as a medium to reveal, explain, and ultimately reverse the historical exploitation of women. And they are motivated, as well, by a desire to draw attention to women's causes.

Their successes have been impressive. Anthologies, which in the past have neglected works by important women writers, now include them. Leaders in the field of education now encourage, sometimes insist, that works by women writers be included on course syllabi.

Feminist critics have also provided new insights into works of literature by focusing on the role women play in these works and by illustrating how depictions of stereotypical roles determine the woman's place, how she looks at herself, and how other characters respond and react to her.

Bobbie Ann Mason, Shiloh

"Shiloh" is a story about a young couple whose marriage is on the rocks. The husband, Leroy, was a trucker, but, because of an accident, he cannot drive any longer, and he remains home. Tensions, hidden while Leroy spent so much time on the road, begin to surface as Leroy and his wife, Norma Jean, now spend so much time together. Norma Jean and Leroy were married when they were eighteen and Norma Jean was pregnant. The baby died of sudden infant death syndrome. They have been married for sixteen years, but they have never confronted together the pain of their baby's death, and it remains an unspoken source of guilt. Leroy wants the relationship to work and dreams of building a log cabin for the two of them to settle down in. Norma Jean does not share Leroy's interest in building a log cabin. She has a job, she is getting herself physically fit, and she has started attending classes at the local community college. She is beginning to distance herself from her husband and from her domineering mother, Mabel, as well. On a day trip to Shiloh, site of a famous Civil War battle and now a tourist spot, Norma Jean tells Leroy the marriage is over.

Male and female readers tend to read "Shiloh" somewhat differently, the differences being most obvious in responses to the character of Leroy. Men tend to have some sympathy for Leroy. His log cabin might be more than a pipe dream if Norma Jean showed some interest and offered some support, instead of mocking him and insisting it can't be done. Leroy is trying; he appears more willing than Norma Jean to confront and talk about the main problem within the marriage: the unresolved emotional trauma caused by the baby's death.

Women readers tend to have less sympathy for Leroy. He won't look for work. He smokes too much marijuana. His log cabin is a game, a grown man's Lego set. He is thirty-four years old, but he is still acting like an eighteen-year-old. Norma Jean has to leave him so she can realize her own potential.

Feminist readers would also condemn Leroy as a husband who is threatened by his wife's tentative steps toward emancipation, a man who tries to resubjugate his wife by promising to build her a log cabin. The log cabin is a symbol of the material security men are supposed to provide for women, but, typically, a false symbol, existing only on paper and as a replica Leroy builds from Popsicle sticks. Moreover, none of the town's subdivisions will even permit the construction of a log cabin.

Feminist readers would also attack Norma Jean's mother, Mabel, as an accessory to the perpetuation of a male-dominated world. Mabel inspects Norma Jean's house and monitors her cooking to make sure her daughter fulfills her gender roles as a good wife and housekeeper. She refuses to let her thirty-four-year-old daughter smoke and punishes her when she catches Norma Jean doing so. Indeed, it is this episode that pushes Norma Jean over the edge and gives her the courage to leave her husband and stand up to her mother. At Shiloh, Norma Jean tells Leroy things changed when Mabel caught her smoking. "That set something off," she says. Here Norma Jean's feminist consciousness, suppressed throughout the story, surfaces clearly and powerfully. Early feminists declared their emancipation by smoking openly. By refusing to allow her mother, a symbol of an outmoded approach to gender roles, to stop her from smoking, Norma Jean establishes her own feminist credentials. She becomes truly emancipated. She wins the civil war, which Mason symbolizes by setting the end of the story in Shiloh and by taking the town's name for her story's title. Norma Jean is free now to strike out on her own and fulfill her true role as a modern emancipated woman.

Andrew Marvel, To His Coy Mistress

The narrator of "To His Coy Mistress" is a stereotypical male trying to sweet-talk a young woman into having a sexual relationship with him. He has propositioned the young woman who has refused, saying now is not the right time. The narrator does not know that no means no.

The narrator argues that life is short, and that we need to seize the opportunity for pleasure when we are young because youth is so transitory. He lavishes praise on the young woman's beauty, praising her eyes, her skin, and her breasts. He warns her that her beauty will fade as she ages and that she will not be as desirable as she is now. He is very clear about what he wants from this young woman. He does not want a relationship; he wants sex.

Marvel's poem depicts one of the clearest cases of sexual harassment in all of Western literature. His narrator says nothing about the woman's character. He shows no interest in her conversation, in her values, in her opinions on anything. He assumes she will consent. He spends all his time and energy browbeating her into bed with what he imagines to be a silver tongue, but which is, in reality, frequently crude imagery:

> . . . then worms shall try
> That long-preserved virginity,
> (lines 27–28)

> The grave's a fine and private place,
> But none I think do there embrace.
> (lines 31–32)

Typically, he dismisses her refusal to have sex with him as coyness, not disinterest. His male ego prevents him from realizing the young woman may not want to have a sexual relationship with him. He assumes her coyness is her consent. He is the stereotypical young man whose pride drowns out a young woman's rejection.

Kate Chopin, The Story of an Hour

In Chopin's story, a rather fragile young woman, Louise Mallard, is told of her husband's death in a train accident. At first she is devastated but she soon realizes she can now look forward to a life of freedom and her despair turns into exaltation. She has felt oppressed within her marriage, even though her husband has always treated her kindly. But at the end of the story her husband arrives home, very much alive, having escaped the tragedy. Louise's already weak heart cannot endure the shock, and she dies.

"The Story of an Hour" illustrates the extent to which marriage represses a woman's freedom. Louise rejoices, not because she believes her husband has died, but because she has been given a chance at independence and freedom. "There would be no one to live for during those coming years," she reflects after the news has sunk in; "she would live for herself." Ironically, she whispers a prayer for a long life. Ironically, the doctors conclude that the overwhelming joy of seeing her husband alive caused her heart attack.

Her heart attack is caused less by the shock or the joy of seeing her husband alive than by the distress she experiences as she realizes her chance for a new life has been dashed. Louise was about to acquire a will of her own. The knowledge that she again will have to subvert her own will to that of her husband proves to be too much for her to bear.

GAY/LESBIAN CRITICISM

Like Marxists and feminists, gay/lesbian critics are a special-interest subgroup of the reader-response school. They are committed to adding the work of gay and lesbian writers to the canon of widely studied poems and stories, so these works will be read and appreciated by all readers. They are committed to revealing hitherto neglected but implicit homosexual relationships between and among characters in literary works and to revealing how this implicit homosexuality affects meaning. They are committed to revealing the homophobia inherent in many canonical works. And they are committed to agitate, through literary criticism, for increased civil rights for gay and lesbian people.

Willa Cather, Paul's Case

"Paul's Case" was written around the turn of the last century, but other Pauls can still be found today in any American high school. Paul is that teenage boy who is persecuted by his peers and his family because he is different. Paul is homosexual and cannot conform to a straight world.

Cather, who was herself gay, depicts Paul as a rather stereotypical homosexual. He wears elegant, colorful clothing. He loves theater and music and enjoys his work as an usher at a concert hall. He rebels against the constraints of school. Paul's stern father, unable to understand his son's behavior and worried about his inability to conform, makes Paul get a job and forbids him to visit the theater or go to concerts. Paul steals money from his employer and moves away from Pittsburgh to New York. He checks into the Waldorf, buys fine new clothes, and goes to concerts. It is possible that he has a relationship with a Yale freshman whom he meets at the hotel. They spend a night on the town together, but they do not part on friendly terms. Cather wrote this story, of course, at a time when it would simply not be acceptable to describe a homosexual relationship in anything other than oblique terms. On the eighth day of his fantasy visit to New York, Paul reads in the Pittsburgh papers that his father has paid back the money Paul had stolen and is on his way to New York to bring his son back to Pittsburgh. This Paul cannot face. He commits suicide by hurling himself into an oncoming train.

An adolescent boy commits suicide because he cannot live in a world that cannot accept his sexuality. Cather's story is almost a hundred years old, but its plot and its theme remain familiar.

DECONSTRUCTION

Deconstruction is a form of literary analysis that takes the subjectivity of interpretation to its extreme. Reader-response theory asserts that the understanding of a text is mediated by the reader's gender, political philosophy, sexual orientation, ethnic origin. As deconstruction critics point out, language is, by nature, arbitrary and ambiguous. If different people interpret different texts in so many different yet legitimate ways, language is obviously an imperfect signifier of meaning. A single true meaning is unknowable.

Deconstruction critics take this notion as their starting point and "interrogate a text" to point out how the meaning of a text inevitably deconstructs or breaks down. New

Critics and Structuralists read a text closely to show how the parts, how the author's technique, create a unified and harmonious whole. Deconstructionists read a text closely to prove the opposite: to show how the parts are at war with each other, how the technique fails to establish meaning. "All interpretation," the deconstructionists argue, "is misinterpretation."

Deconstruction critics, therefore, do not allow for a privileged or even a reasonable reading. Indeed, they take special pride in refuting privileged interpretations, which tend to exonerate conservative attitudes embedded in texts: the subjugation of women and minorities, the inequitable distribution of wealth, the class system. Deconstruction critics tend to be political radicals.

They are linguistic radicals as well, in their belief that words have only relative meaning. The meaning of the word "hot," for example, is relative. A hot day is 90 degrees, but 90 degrees would be the temperature of a cool oven. Absolute meaning within a collection of related words, a text, is always elusive. All readings are unreasonable.

William Wordsworth, Daffodils (I Wandered Lonely as a Cloud)

Most critics interpret Wordsworth's poem in light of the poet's famous comment in his Preface to his *Lyrical Ballads* (1798), where he notes the connection between the poetic process and the joy of "emotion recollected in tranquility." The joy is an experience he had on a walk when he saw "A host, of golden daffodils" (line 4) beside a lake. He was struck by the beauty of the scene and by the pleasure it brought to him. He thought his joy would be transitory but even now, he writes in the fourth and final stanza, he will, when "In vacant or in pensive mood" (line 19), remember the daffodils and his heart will fill with pleasure.

The problem with this reading is that Wordsworth's diction undercuts any sense of joy the experience with the daffodils supposedly gave him. The third word in the poem is "lonely," an adverb Wordsworth uses to describe his walk. "Lonely" connotes sorrow rather than joy. He goes on to say the flowers seemed endless, "Continuous as the stars that shine" (line 7). But stars do not shine continuously; they shine only at night. They may emanate light all of the time but they "shine" only when surrounded by the contrasting dark. The diction is also childish—"twinkle," "sprightly," "glee"—and hence the images the diction creates are also childish. We are left with the picture of a lonely poet, not tiptoeing through the tulips exactly, but skipping through a field of daffodils, trying to be happy, but succeeding only in looking foolish.

In the final stanza, he is lying on his couch "In vacant or in pensive mood" (line 19) and reliving the joy he experienced in the past as he appreciated the beauty of the daffodils. It is hard for the reader to share that beauty, given the way the poet describes it. Again, the diction undercuts any sense of seriousness. The poet does not have an open mind; he has a "vacant" mind.

"Daffodils" is clearly a parody of the romantic poet, sighing longingly over the beauty of nature, oblivious to the harshness of the real world, which unfolds around him.

Flannery O'Connor, A Good Man Is Hard to Find

O'Connor insists that her stories are the product of her religious devotion and that they are written primarily to illustrate the power and the glory of divine grace. "A Good Man Is Hard to Find," then, is, ostensibly, a story about an old woman who saves the soul of a serial killer, or at least begins the process of doing so, by sharing with him her Christian compassion.

The old woman, identified only as the "grandmother," is on a road trip with her son and his family. She has read in the papers about the "Misfit," a serial killer on the loose. She insists her son drive down a deserted road so that she can see a particularly beautiful house she remembers as a child. They have an accident and, inevitably, meet up with the serial killer and his two partners. The two partners kill mom, dad, and the three children. Grandmother begs for her life, pleads with the Misfit to pray, and actually reaches out to touch him. He shoots her three times in the heart. But the tragedy of her death is mitigated by the blossoming of her own Christian compassion and by hints that the Misfit is beginning to see the error of his ways and is thinking about reforming.

Or so O'Connor would have us believe. Unfortunately, her thesis is undercut by the grandmother's character. Throughout the story, the grandmother has been portrayed as a rather unpleasant, mean-spirited, and domineering woman. She is certainly racist, as her comments about African Americans make clear. Her religious devotion is hypocritical. Her Christian compassion, because it is insincere, fails to move the Misfit. Grandmother is trying to save her own skin, not reform a serial killer. When she reaches out to touch the Misfit, in a last desperate effort to save herself, he "sprang back as if a snake had bitten him." The reference to the snake, the symbol of Satan, suggests the grandmother's duplicity. The Misfit does not respond positively to the grandmother and consider the error of his ways, as O'Connor would have us believe. Indeed, he kills her the second she touches him and comments "She would have been a good woman . . . if it had been somebody there to shoot her every minute of her life." He recognizes her for what she is: not a good Christian woman but a hypocritical coward. A close reading of "A Good Man Is Hard to Find" reveals a story that is much more nihilistic than Christian, despite the convictions of its author.

NEW HISTORICISM

New historicist critics believe that a literary work is the product of a culture. (Their method is often referred to as Cultural Studies). A culture is composed of people living under certain social, political, philosophical, economic, and intellectual systems. This culture, through the author as an agent of the culture, produces a literary work. To understand the literary work, therefore, the reader must understand the culture that produced it.

New historicism is an interdisciplinary approach to interpreting a literary text. The reader must know the political, the economic, the psychological, the social, the philosophical, the scientific assumptions and conditions within which the author was working and read the author's work in light of those assumptions and conditions. In any culture, of course, there are competing political and social systems. Wealth is distributed inequitably, hence political power and social power are distributed inequitably. New historicists examine the tensions and conflicts that competing social and political forces cause within the culture in which the author was working, and interpret literature within this context.

New historicists use all methods of literary analysis in combination but, because they are especially interested in cultural conflicts, they tend to favor those methods that will most help them examine the tensions within a culture. Marxism, feminism, gay/lesbian, and other politically radical methods of analysis have most influenced new historicist critics. Similarly, because they believe such social conflict creates textual conflict, they are drawn to deconstruction as a method of textual analysis.

This focus on Marxism and feminism generally reveals widespread social injustice within cultures as reflected in literary works. New historicism is ultimately political, using, as it does, literary criticism as a means of promoting social justice.

Charlotte Perkins Gilman, The Yellow Wallpaper

"The Yellow Wallpaper" was written around 1890, a time when women revered and respected the opinions of men (male physicians, especially) to a greater extent than they do today. It was also written at a time when the treatment of depression was, measured by today's standards, unenlightened. The most common treatment was the one prescribed by a Philadelphia physician, S. Weir Mitchell, who insisted depressed patients would be cured if they were confined to bed, ate more than usual, took iron supplements, some exercise, some massage, and even some electric shock therapy. These cultural attitudes that viewed women as the weaker sex and a woman's emotional problems as hysteria to be treated in the way Dr. Mitchell prescribed, mediate the theme and the plot of Gilman's story.

The narrator of the story is suffering, apparently from postpartum depression. Her physician husband, in keeping with methods of treating depression approved of at this time, confines her to a room in a colonial mansion. She is to do nothing but rest. She is a writer, but her husband won't let her write because he thinks the mental strain will worsen her condition. But she writes of her experience confined in the house. She is the story's narrator.

Alone in her room much of the time, the narrator begins to dwell, in an unhealthy way, on the ugly yellow wallpaper that surrounds her. She begins to see strange shapes and human forms blending in with the wallpaper's pattern. Her husband threatens to send her to see Dr. Mitchell. She wants to leave the house, but her husband refuses. He is tender to her, not cruel; he simply believes he is doing the right thing. And she defers to him, as her role as wife dictates that she should. But her condition continues to deteriorate. She continues to watch the wallpaper, which seems to come alive with various shapes and forms. She imagines the pattern is of bars, a symbol of her imprisonment. She imagines there is a woman behind the wallpaper. The woman takes hold of the bars, shakes them, and tries to climb through them. She seems to succeed and she creeps around the house and the garden outside. What is really happening, of course, is that the narrator's depression is morphing into psychosis. At the end of the story, she locks herself into her room and relentlessly peels away at the yellow wallpaper, frightening even her husband to the point that he faints when he realizes the full extent of her emotional transformation.

The narrator is very much a product of her time and place. To regain her emotional stability, she needs to be active and engaged in the kind of productive work she enjoyed as a writer. But the role society has placed upon her, as an upper-middle-class late-Victorian housewife, combined with a counterproductive method of treating depression, obviates any chance she has for happiness. "The Yellow Wallpaper" is a critique of a culture that subjugates women and that treats the mentally ill as if they are disobedient children.

Amy Tan, A Pair of Tickets

In "A Pair of Tickets" a young Chinese American girl travels to China to meet her half-sisters, twins whom her now dead mother had to abandon during the Japanese invasion in 1944. Born and raised in America, Jing-Mei had never considered herself Chinese. But as she leaves Hong Kong and arrives in Shenzhen, she is instantly aware of her Chinese identity. This sense of her Chinese identity intensifies as she meets her native Chinese family, especially her twin half-sisters with whom she instantly bonds, "all hesitations and expectations forgotten." Jing-Mei's mother was right: Her Chinese identity "is in your blood, waiting to let go." Jing-Mei's father takes a Polaroid of the three girls together, and, as they watch it develop before their eyes, they see, in their combined images, the face of their mother.

"A Pair of Tickets" tells readers the extent to which ethnicity determines identity. Readers who are members of ethnic minorities, especially those who have visited homelands and who have met or been reunited with family, will read "A Pair of Tickets" as insiders. They will identify with Jing-Mei and understand how much her experience in China means to her self-understanding and awareness. Other readers will have a different, but no less profound response. They will gain some insight into the difficulties their friends and neighbors, who are members of ethnic minorities, face adjusting and adapting to "mainstream" society when their names and faces reveal their minority status. They learn, as well, how central a role ethnic identity plays in shaping the characters of these friends and neighbors. This response will evoke more envy than concern. In the course of the story, Jing-Mei loses nothing of her American heritage and identity, but she gains a whole new heritage and identity. Everyone should be so lucky.

Credits

Author–Title Index

A Good Man Is Hard to Find, 165–66

A Midsummer Night's Dream, 87–89

A Pair of Tickets, 168

A Poison Tree, 116–17

A Refusal to Mourn, 105–6

A Rose for Emily, 40–41

A Slumber Did My Spirit Seal, 14–15

A Supermarket in California, 158–59

A Time Past, 110

A Valediction: Forbidding Mourning, 114

Ackerman, Diane, Beija Flor, 120

Adonais, 29

All Gone, 42–43

Among School Children, 142

Anderson, Sherwood, I'm a Fool, 54

An Occurrence at Owl Creek Bridge, 118–19

An Old-Fashioned Story, 47–48

Anthem for Doomed Youth, 17

Araby, 130–31

Arnold, Matthew, Dover Beach, 19

At the San Francisco Airport, 86–87

Atwood, Margaret, Rape Fantasies, 70–71

Auden, W. H., In Memory of W. B. Yeats, 29–30

Austen, Jane, Pride and Prejudice, 9–11

A Worn Path, 60

Babylon Revisited, 69–70

Barn Burning, 155

Barrett Browning, Elizabeth, How Do I Love Thee, 95

Bartleby, The Scrivener, 53

Batter My Heart, Three-Personed God, 106–7

Because I Could Not Stop for Death, 106

Beckett, Samuel, Krapp's Last Tape, 58

Waiting for Godot, 36–37

Beija Flor, 120

Beyond the Pale, 78–79

Bishop, Elizabeth, The Fish, 46

Bierce, Ambrose, An Occurrence at Owl Creek Bridge, 118–19

Bitch, 42

Blake, William, A Poison Tree, 116–17

London, 81–82

The Sick Rose, 129

The Tyger, 15

Bleak House, 75–76

Boys and Girls, 71–72

Brideshead Revisited, 122–24

Bright Star, 136

Browning, Elizabeth Barrett, How Do I Love Thee, 95

Browning, Robert, My Last Duchess, 56–57

Porphyria's Lover, 79–80

Bunyan, John, Pilgrim's Progress, 133–34

Byron, George Gordon, Lord, The Destruction of Sennacherib, 15–16

She Walks in Beauty, 120

Byzantium, 104–5

Carver, Raymond, Neighbors, 8–9

Catch 22, 99–101

Cather, Willa, Paul's Case, 163

Cheever, John, The Swimmer, 132

Chesterton, G. K., The Donkey, 139

Chopin, Kate, The Awakening, 11–12

The Storm, 66–67

The Story of an Hour, 162

Church Going, 106

Clay, 112–13

Cohen, Leonard, Dance Me To The End of Love, 95

Coleridge, Samuel Taylor, Kubla Khan, 1

The Rime of the Ancient Mariner, 23–24

Colwin, Laurie, An Old-Fashioned Story, 47–48

Conrad, Joseph, Heart of
    Darkness, 44–45
Crane Stephen, The Blue Hotel,
    151–52
    The Bride Comes to Yellow
    Sky, 67–68
Cummings, E.E., somewhere i
    have never travelled, 95–96
Daffodils, 164–165
Dance Me To The End of Love, 95
Death Be Not Proud, 105
Desert Places, 117
Dickens, Charles, Bleak House,
    75–76
Dickinson, Emily, Because I
    Could Not Stop for Death,
    106
    I Heard a Fly Buzz, 128–29
    I Like to See It Lap the Miles,
    156–57
    I Taste a Liquor, 104
    My Life Had Stood a Loaded
    Gun, 126–27
    There's a Certain Slant of
    Light, 117
Directive, 45
Disillusionment of Ten o'Clock,
    19–20
Dixon, Stephen, All Gone, 42–43
Do Not Go Gentle, 25–26
Donne, John, A Valediction:
    Forbidding Mourning, 114
    Batter My Heart, Three-
    Personed God, 106–7
    Death Be Not Proud, 105
    The Flea, 113–14
Dover Beach, 19
Dubus, Andre, The Curse, 41–42
Dulce et Decorum Est, 139
Dunne, Stephen, Tenderness,
    139–40
Eberhart, Richard, The Fury of
    Aerial Bombardment, 102
Eliot, T. S., The Love Song of
    J. Alfred Prufrock, 54–55
    The Wasteland, 83–85
Eve, 15
Eveline, 68–69
Everyday Use, 62–63
Faulkner, William, A Rose for
    Emily, 40–41
    Barn Burning, 155
Fern Hill, 122
Fire and Ice, 128
Fitzgerald, F. Scott, Babylon
    Revisited, 69–70
    The Great Gatsby, 57–58

Frost, Robert, Directive, 45
    Desert Places, 117
    Fire and Ice, 128
    Stopping by Woods on a
    Snowy Evening, 80
Full Many a Glorious Morning,
    85–86
Futility, 97
Gilman, Charlotte Perkins, The
    Yellow Wallpaper, 167–68
Ginsberg, Allen, A Supermarket
    in California, 158–59
Girl, 93
Giovanni, Nikki, Woman, 137
God's Grandeur, 17
Guests of the Nation, 6, 51
Hamlet, 32–34
Hardy, Thomas, The Darkling
    Thrush, 86
    The Ruined Maid, 47
Harrison Bergeron, 63–64
Hawthorne, Nathaniel, Young
    Goodman Brown, 133–34
Hayden, Robert, Those Winter
    Sundays, 72–73
Heart of Darkness, 44–45
Heller, Joseph, Catch 22,
    99–101
Hemingway, Ernest, Hills Like
    White Elephants, 74
    The Snows of Kilimanjaro, 81
Her First Ball, 55–56
Herrick, Robert, To the Virgins
    to Make Much of Time, 109
Herbert, George, The Collar,
    107–8
Hills Like White Elephants, 74
Hodgson, Ralph, Eve, 16
Home Soil, 101–2
Homer, The Iliad, 28, 115
    The Odyssey, 18, 28
Hope, A.D., Imperial Adam, 119
Hopkins, Gerard Manly, God's
    Grandeur, 17
Housman, A. E., Loveliest of
    Trees, 109–10
How Do I Love Thee, 95
How to Become a Writer, 138
I Heard a Fly Buzz, 128–29
I Like to See It Lap the Miles,
    156–57
I Stand Here Ironing, 158
I Taste a Liquor, 104
I'm a Fool, 54
Imperial Adam, 119
In a Station of the Metro, 125
In Memoriam, 29

In Memory of W.B. Yeats, 29–30

Jackson, Shirley, The Lottery, 82–83

James, Henry, The Turn of the Screw, 153

Jarrell, Randall, The Death of the Ball Turret Gunner, 99

Jonson, Ben, Still to be Neat, 121–22

Joyce, James, Araby, 130–31
Clay, 112–13
The Dead, 120–21
Eveline, 68–69

Keats, John, Adonais, 29
Bright Star, 136
La Belle Dame Sans Merci, 149–50
Ode on a Grecian Urn, 127–28
Ode to a Nightingale, 26–27
On First Looking into Chapman's Homer, 115
To Autumn, 102–3

Kincaid, Jamaica, Girl, 93
What I Have Been Doing Lately, 7–8

Kizer, Carolyn, Bitch, 42

Krapp's Last Tape, 58

Kubla Khan, 1–3

Kumin, Maxine, Morning Swim, 103–4
Woodchucks, 48–49

La Belle Dame Sans Merci, 149–50

Larkin, Philip, Church Going, 107

Lawrence, D.H., The Horse Dealer's Daughter, 96–97
The Odour of Chrysanthemums, 52
The Rocking Horse Winner, 66

Leda and the Swan, 22

Lessing, Doris, Our Friend Judith, 73–74

Levertov, Denise, A Time Past, 110
What Were They Like, 97–98

Livvie, 132–33

Living in Sin, 39

London, 81–82

Lovelace, Richard, To Althea from Prison, 141–42
To Lucasta, On Going to the Wars, 143–44

Loveliest of Trees, 109–10

Lycidas, 29

Mason, Bobbie Ann, Shiloh, 159–61

Mansfield, Katherine, Her First Ball, 55–56
The Daughters of the Late Colonel, 92
The Garden Party, 38–39
Miss Brill, 136

Marvell, Andrew, To His Coy Mistress, 161–62

Melville, Herman, Bartleby, the Scrivener, 53

Merwin, W.S., Separation, 115

Methought I Saw My Late Espouséd Saint, 143

Millay, Edna St. Vincent, What Lips My Lips Have Kissed, 110

Mirror, 127

Milton, John, Lycidas, 29
Methought I Saw My Late Espouséd Saint, 143
On His Blindness, 21–22
On the Late Massacre at Piedmont, 146–47
Paradise Lost, 28–29
When I Consider How My Light Is Spent, 21–22

Moore, Lorrie, How to Become a Writer, 138

Miss Brill, 136

Morning Swim, 103–4

Munro, Alice, Boys and Girls, 71–72
The Found Boat, 39–40

My Last Duchess, 56–57

My Live Had Stood, A Loaded Gun, 126–27

My Mistress's Eyes Are Nothing Like the Sun, 116

My Papa's Waltz, 91–92

Naming of Parts, 82

Neighbors, 8–9

No One's a Mystery, 6–7

Not Marble Nor the Gilded Monuments, 21

Not Waving but Drowning, 112

O'Brien, Tim, The Things They Carried, 98

O'Connor, Flannery, A Good Man Is Hard to Find, 165–66

O'Connor, Frank, Guests of the Nation, 6, 51

Ode: Intimations of Immortality, 27–28

Ode on a Grecian Urn, 127–28

Ode to a Nightingale, 26–27

Olds, Sharon, The Planned Child, 94

Olsen, Tillie, I Stand Here Ironing, 158

On First Looking into Chapman's Homer, 115

On His Blindness, 21–22

On the Late Massacre at Piedmont, 146–47

Othello, 49–50

One Perfect Rose, 138

Our Friend Judith, 73–74

Owen, Wilfred, Anthem for Doomed Youth, 17
  Dulce et Decorum Est, 139
  Futility, 97

Paradise Lost, 28–29

Parker, Dorothy, One Perfect Rose, 138

Paul's Case, 163

Piercy, Marge, Wellfleet Sabbath, 124

Pilgrim's Progress, 133–34

Plath, Sylvia, Mirror, 127

Poe, Edgar Allan, The Cask of Amontillado, 153–54
  The Masque of the Red Death, 115–16

Poor Soul the Center of My Sinful Earth, 105

Pope, Alexander, The Rape of the Lock, 145–46

Porphyria's Lover, 79–80

Porter, Katherine Anne, The Jilting of Granny Weatherall, 59

Pound, Ezra, In a Station of the Metro, 125

Pride and Prejudice, 9–11

Pygmalion, 61–62

Randall, Dudley, The Ballad of Birmingham, 24–25

Rape Fantasies, 70–71

Reed, Henry, Naming of Parts, 82

Rich, Adrienne, Living in Sin, 39

Richard Cory, 60

Robinson, E. A., Richard Cory, 60

Roethke, Theodore, My Papa's Waltz, 91–92

Ross, Sinclair, The Painted Door, 77–78

Sailing to Byzantium, 104–5

Separation, 115

Shakespeare, William
  A Midsummer Night's Dream, 87–89
  Full Many a Glorious Morning, 85–86

Hamlet, 32–34
  My Mistress's Eyes Are Nothing Like the Sun, 116
  Not Marble Nor the Gilded Monuments, 21
  Othello, 49–50
  Poor Soul, The Center of My Sinful Earth, 105
  That Time of Year Thou Mayest in Me Behold, 112
  Two Loves I Have of Comfort and Despair, 61
  When in Disgrace with Fortune, 20
  When My Love Swears That She Is Made of Truth, 137

Shaw, George Bernard, Pygmalion, 61–62

She Walks in Beauty, 120

Shiloh, 159–61

Shelley, Percy Byshe, Adonais, 29

Smith, A. J. M., The Lonely Land, 103

Smith, Stevie, Not Waving but Drowning, 112

Somewhere i have never travelled, 95–96

Steinbeck, John, The Chrysanthemums, 129–30

Stevens, Wallace, Disillusionment of Ten o'Clock, 19–20
  Sunday Morning, 108–9

Still to be Neat, 121–22

St. Luke, The Parable of the Prodigal Son, 90–91

Stopping by Woods on a Snowy Evening, 80

Sunday Morning, 108–9

Talent, Elizabeth, No One's a Mystery, 6–7

Tan, Amy, A Pair of Tickets, 168
  Two Kinds, 93–94

Tenderness, 139–40

Tennyson, Alfred Lord, In Memoriam, 29
  Tithonus, 30
  Ulysses, 18

That Time of Year Thou Mayest in Me Behold, 112

The A & P, 8

The Aeneid, 28

The Awakening, 11–12

The Ballad of Birmingham, 24–25

The Blue Hotel, 151–52
The Bride Comes to Yellow Sky, 67–68
The Cask of Amontillado, 153–54
The Catbird Seat, 46
The Chrysanthemums, 129–30
The Collar, 107–8
The Curse, 41–42
The Daughters of the Late Colonel, 92
The Darkling Thrush, 86
The Dead, 120–21
The Death of the Ball Turret Gunner, 99
The Destruction of Sennacherib, 15–16
The Donkey, 139
The Fish, 46
The Flea, 113–14
The Folly of Being Comforted, 96
The Force that Through the Green Fuse, 129
The Found Boat, 39–40
The Fury of Aerial Bombardment, 102
The Garden Party, 38–39
The Great Gatsby, 57–58
The Horse Dealer's Daughter, 96–97
The Iliad, 28, 115
The Importance of Being Earnest, 34–35
The Jilting of Granny Weatherall, 59
The Masque of the Red Death, 115–16
The Lonely Land, 103
The Lottery, 82–83
The Love Song of J. Alfred Prufrock, 54–55
The Odor of Chrysanthemums, 52
The Odyssey, 18, 28
The Painted Door, 77–78
The Parable of the Prodigal Son, 90–91
The Planned Child, 94
The Rape of the Lock, 145–46
The Red Wheelbarrow, 124–25
The Rime of the Ancient Mariner, 23–24
The Rocking Horse Winner, 66
The Ruined Maid, 47
The Second Coming, 131
The Sick Rose, 129
The Snows of Kilimanjaro, 81

The Storm, 66–67
The Story of an Hour, 162
The Swimmer, 132
The Things They Carried, 98
The Turn of the Screw, 153
The Tyger, 15
The Waste Land, 83–85
The Writer, 92–93
The Yellow Wallpaper, 167–68
There's a Certain Slant of Light, 117
Thomas, Dylan, A Refusal to Mourn, 105–6
    Do Not Go Gentle, 25–26
    Fern Hill, 122
    The Force that Through the Green Fuse, 129
Those Winter Sundays, 72–73
Thurber, James, The Catbird Seat, 46
Tithonus, 30
To Althea From Prison, 141–42
To His Coy Mistress, 161–62
To Lucasta, On Going to the Wars, 143–44
To the Virgins, To Make Much of Time, 109
To Autumn, 102–3
Two Kinds, 93–94
Two Loves I Have of Comfort and Despair, 61
Trevor, William, Beyond the Pale, 78–79
Ulysses, 18
Updike, John, The A & P, 8
Virgil, The Aeneid, 28
Vonnegut, Kurt, Harrison Bergeron, 63–64
Waiting for Godot, 36–37
Walker, Alice, Everyday Use, 62–63
    Brideshead Revisited, 122–24
Wellfleet Sabbath, 124
Welty, Eudora, A Worn Path, 60
Welty, Eudora, Livvie, 132–33
What Lips My Lips Have Kissed, 110
What Were They Like, 97–98
When I Consider How My Light Is Spent, 21–22
When in Disgrace With Fortune, 20
When My Love Swears that She Is Made of Truth, 137
When You Are Old, 135–36
Wilber, Richard, The Writer, 92–93

Wilde, Oscar, The Importance of
    Being Earnest, 34–35
Williams, William Carlos, The
    Red Wheelbarrow, 124–25
Winters, Yvor, At the San
    Francisco Airport, 86–87
Woodchucks, 48–49
Wordsworth, William, A
    Slumber Did My Spirit Seal,
    14–15
  Daffodils, 164–65
  Ode: Intimations of Immor-
    tality, 27–28

Woman, 137
Yeats, William Butler, Among
    School Children, 142
  Byzantium, 104–5
  Leda and the Swan, 22
  Sailing to Byzantium, 104–5
  The Folly of Being Comforted,
    96
  The Second Coming, 131
  When You Are Old, 135–36
Young Goodman Brown, 133–34
Zabytko, Irene, Home Soil, 101–2
Allegory, 33

Literary Term Index

Alliteration, 17
Anapestic, 14, 15
Antagonist, 5
Archetype, 43
Assonance, 17
Ballad, 22
Blank verse, 18
Blocking agent, 34
Carpe diem, 109
Catharsis, 32
Character, 51, 111, 120, 131
Comedy, 34
Coming-of-age story, 71
Conceit, 114
Contextual symbol, 126
Couplet, 13
Cultural symbol, 126
Dactylic, 14, 16
Deconstruction, 163
Drama, 31
Dramatic irony, 47, 49
Dramatic monologue, 30
Dynamic character, 51
Elegy, 29
Epic, 28
Epiphany, 6
Eye rhyme, 14
Fable, 66
Fiction, 5
First-person major-character
    narrator, 65, 70
First-person minor-character
    narrator, 65, 73
Flashback, 40
Flat character, 51, 54
Free verse, 18
Full rhyme, 14
Haiku, 124
Half rhyme, 14
Hamartia, 31
Hyperbole, 111
Iambic, 14
Imagery, 118
Imagism/Imagist, 124
In medias res, 28
Irony, 47, 49, 51, 59, 82, 138
Limited-omniscient narrator, 65,
    68
Litotes, 111

Literature, 1, 3
Metaphor, 85, 111
Metonomy, 111
Multiple points of view, 74
Novel, 9
Narrative, 5
Octave, 13
Non-sequential plot, 38, 40
Novella, 11
Objective point-of-view, 65,
    74
Ode, 26
Omniscient narrator, 65
Paradox, 106
Pastoral elegy, 29
Personification, 111
Petrarchan sonnet, 21
Plot, 38, 77, 118
Plot twist, 45
Poetry, 13
Point of view, 65
Protagonist, 5
Quatrain, 13
Reader-response criticism,
    155–56
Regular verse, 13
Rhyme scheme, 13
Rhyming couplet, 13
Rhythm patterns, 14
Round character, 51
Satire, 61
Scapegoat, 32
Sestet, 13
Sequential plot, 38
Setting, 77, 122
Shakespearean sonnet, 20
Short story, 5
Sight rhyme, 14
Simile, 111
Sonnet, 20
Spondee, 14, 17
Static character, 51, 54
Stereotype, 34, 51, 56
Symbolism, 80, 116, 126
Synecdoche, 111
Tercet, 13
Theater of the Absurd, 35
Theme, 90, 114, 124

Tone, 135
Tragedy, 31
Tragic flaw, 31
Tragic hero, 31

Trochaic, 14, 15
Universal symbol, 126
Varied rhythm and meter, 16
Villanelle, 25